BUSINESS ISSUES, COMPETITION AND ENTREPRENEURSHIP

T0294991

VENTURE CAPITAL AND ANGEL INVESTING

BUSINESS ISSUES, COMPETITION AND ENTREPRENEURSHIP

Additional books in this series can be found on Nova's website under the Series tab.

Additional E-books in this series can be found on Nova's website under the E-books tab.

BUSINESS ISSUES, COMPETITION AND ENTREPRENEURSHIP

VENTURE CAPITAL AND ANGEL INVESTING

ANDREW M. LANE

AND

NICOLE P. MIFFLIN

EDITORS

Nova Science Publishers, Inc.

New York

Library of Congress Cataloging-in-Publication Data

Venture capital and angel investing / editors, Andrew M. Lane and Nicole P. Mifflin.
    p. cm.
  Includes index.
  ISBN 978-1-61324-122-6 (softcover)
  1. New business enterprises--United States--Finance. 2. Small business--United States--Finance. 3. Venture capital--United States. 4. Investments--United States. I. Lane, Andrew M. II. Mifflin, Nicole P.
  HG4027.6.V46 2011
  332'.04154--dc22
                        2011008488

Published by Nova Science Publishers, Inc. + New York

CONTENTS

PREFACE

Entrepreneurs constantly seek capital for new and existing ventures even though they face considerable constraints in obtaining financing. Venture capital from outside investors has been considered an important driver in the startup and growth of entrepreneurial firms. Unlike venture capital investments, angel investments are made by individual investors who do not make up a known population. Therefore, much of what is reported about angel investing comes from anecdotes and surveys of convenience samples, which are prone to biases and inaccuracies. This new book examines the roles of angel investing in the entrepreneurial finance system and the funded and unfunded business plans to determine the key factors in the venture capital investment decision process.

Chapter 1 - Entrepreneurs constantly seek capital for new and existing ventures although they face considerable constraints in obtaining financing. Venture capital from outside investors has been considered an important driver in the startup and growth of entrepreneurial firms. Understanding the specific investment criteria for venture capital funding is of foremost importance, since this may substantially improve these firms' chances of acquiring funding. The authors have chosen to predict funding by measuring the decisions on both funded and unfunded business plans.

Chapter 2 - Many observers consider angel investments to be one of the key drivers behind the startup and the growth of new businesses, despite a paucity of information to confirm whether or not this is true. Unlike venture capital investments, angel investments are made by individual investors who do not make up a known population. Therefore, much of what is reported about angel investing comes from anecdotes and surveys of convenience samples, which are prone to biases and inaccuracies. Moreover, research on angel investment is plagued by definitional confusion, in which different investigators confound informal investors, friends and family who invest in startups, accredited and unaccredited angel investors, and individual and group investing. The variation makes it difficult to compare findings across studies.

In: Venture Capital and Angel Investing ISBN: 978-1-61324-122-6
Editors: A. M. Lane, N. P. Mifflin © 2011 Nova Science Publishers, Inc.

Chapter 1

UNCOVERING KNOWLEDGE STRUCTURES OF VENTURE CAPITAL INVESTMENT DECISION MAKING[*]

Pankaj Patel and Rodney D'Souza

ABSTRACT

Studies on venture capital (VC) investment decision using espoused criteria and utility aggregation methods have shown mixed results. Using a latent decision structures approach from psychological scaling literature, we reduce random and systematic biases arising from VC decision environment. In addition, we further address such biases using a combination of parametric and nonparametric techniques and practitioner specified decision criteria on 143 funded and nonfunded business plans. Compared to previous studies that have emphasized the central role of the venture team in obtaining funding, we find that (a) a good venture team is critical for not rejecting a business plan but is less critical for funding a business plan (b) a good venture team has decreasing returns even for funded ventures, but favorable competitive conditions and market potential have increasing returns.

Keywords: decision making, entrepreneurship, venture capital

---

[*] This is an edited, reformatted and augmented version of a working paper for Ofiice of Advocacy publication, dated January 2008.

ACKNOWLEDGMENT[1]

This report was developed under a contract with the Small Business Administration, Office of Advocacy, and contains information and analysis that was reviewed and edited by officials of the Office of Advocacy. However, the final conclusions of the report do not necessarily reflect the views of the Office of Advocacy.

The 2008 Office of Advocacy Best Doctoral Paper award was presented to Pankaj Patel and Rodney D'Souza, doctoral students at the University of Louisville, at the United States Association for Small Business and Entrepreneurship (USASBE) annual meeting.

SCOPE AND METHODOLOGY

The authors of this study examined both funded and unfunded business plans to determine the key factors in the venture capital investment decision process. The 2004 sample originally consisted of 200 business plans from venture capitalists that had invested as individuals. Of these business plans, 72 were funded and 128 were not funded. To increase the reliability of the study and obtain equal sized samples, 72 of the 128 unfunded plans were randomly selected. Also, steps were taken to generalize and improve the understanding of the latent decision process used across the United States. This involved obtaining business plans from the East and West Coasts. In a control for industry, business plans only from high technology firms were examined for the year studied.

Analysis was performed in three steps. First, a set of attributes meaningful to VCs was identified using an adapted version of free-listing and focus group sessions. Second, a group of experts was asked to evaluate a set of business plans using the identified attributes. Finally, a Bayesian model was used to

[1] This contract was given to the United States Association for Small Business and Entrepreneurship (USASBE) for a best doctoral student paper award, presented to the awardees at the USASBE annual meeting. This Small Business Research Summary summarizes a research report published by the U.S. Small Business Administration's Office of Advocacy. The opinions and recommendations of the authors of this study do not necessarily reflect official policies of the SBA or other agencies of the U.S. government. For more information, write to the Office of Advocacy at 409 Third Street S.W., Washington DC 20416, or visit the office's website at www.sba.gov/advo.

measure the decision factors that were identified and to predict the VCs' decisions with respect to funding the business plans.

This report was peer reviewed consistent with the Office of Advocacy's data quality guidelines.

PURPOSE

Entrepreneurs constantly seek capital for new and existing ventures although they face considerable constraints in obtaining financing. Venture capital from outside investors has been considered an important driver in the startup and growth of entrepreneurial firms. Understanding the specific investment criteria for venture capital funding is of foremost importance, since this may substantially improve these firms' chances of acquiring funding. The authors have chosen to predict funding by measuring the decisions on both funded and unfunded business plans.

OVERALL FINDINGS

The study posits that venture capitalists (VCs) may be willing to fund a marginal team with better venture potential than a good venture team with limited venture potential. In other words, entrepreneurs need not only to assemble an effective team, but also to clearly demonstrate the venture potential of their proposed business. This finding contrasts with most prior studies, which identify the venture team as the key funding criterion.

Highlights

- The findings suggest that while a venture team's composition and ability are a minimum requirement in the consideration of a venture capital investment and a major factor in explaining why a business plan gets rejected, these features are not significant in explaining why a business plan gets funded.
- The study implies that venture potential is a better indicator of business plan funding than venture team quality and that VCs have

similar knowledge structures and preferences when it comes to funding and not funding actual business plans.

- The researchers analyzed the relationship between rates of return and factors such as venture team quality and venture potential. The analysis finds that a good venture team has decreasing returns even for funded ventures, but favorable competitive conditions and market potential of a business plan have increasing returns.

1. INTRODUCTION

The extant literature on venture capital (VC) funding has found mixed evidence on the relative importance of the venture team, the characteristics of the market, and the business model (Dubini 1989; Hall and Hofer 1993; Macmillan et al. 1985; Macmillan et al. 1987; Shepherd 1999; Tyebjee and Bruno 1984). These findings, however, have been inconsistent mainly due to the fact that: (1) Venture Capitalists (VCs) are often not aware of how they really make judgments (Hall et al. 1993; Zacharakis and Meyer 1998); (2) VCs are affected by high cognitive overloads in decision making due to uncertainty and ambiguity (Camerer and Johnson 1991; Shanteau 1992); (3) VCs suffer from cognitive biases (Shepherd et al. 2003); (4) the assumption that all VCs share similar understanding of the attributes used by researchers (Franke et al. 2006); and (5) researchers have an accurate understanding and knowledge of the number and nature of criteria used by the VCs.

To address the above issues, we start with no assumptions or impositions about the VC decision- making process. In addition, rather than using espoused criteria or hypothetical investment scenarios, we use a set of 143 funded and unfunded business plans for our analysis. We compile a list and the meanings of criteria used by VCs and analyze the role of these criteria on VC decision making using a set of parametric and nonparametric empirical approaches. While previous studies have analyzed VC decision processes through different theoretical lenses, our approach is focused more on knowledge elicitation and representation approaches to address key challenges in the decision making process germane to VCs. Using psychological scaling and expert systems literature, we focus on the nature and structural relationships among the attributes used in making funding decisions. Compared to typical approaches on understanding the nature of decision *processes* that may be fraught with idiosyncratic random or systematic decision errors, we focus on the nature of decision *structures*. Focusing on decision structures may facilitate identification of more stable funding criteria.

This article proceeds as follows. First, we review the literature on expertise and consider VCs to be experts in the realm of investment decision making. We then identify some drawbacks in previous research with regard to elicitation of VC decision making in the light of expertise literature. In the third section, we build our framework – relying on literature from expert knowledge structures to overcome problems associated with knowledge acquisition and representation germane to VC investment decisions. In the fourth section, we describe the data used in the study, followed by the methodologies used to corroborate our analysis framework. Prior literature has typically found the critical role of venture teams in VC funding decisions (Franke et al. 2006). Contrary to these findings, we find that (a) a bad team may definitely lead to nonfunding but a good team does not necessarily lead to funding (b) a good venture team has decreasing returns even for funded ventures, but favorable competitive conditions and market potential have increasing returns. In other words, a good team may be the threshold for being considered for funding but is not a sufficient condition for getting funded. Finally, we discuss the implications of these results for future entrepreneurship research as well as practice.

2. VC's EXPERTISE AND DECISION STRUCTURES

VCs make decisions under conditions of uncertainty, vagueness, and subjectivity of starting a new venture. Such decision making environment may interfere with the power of expertise as seen in more stable domains. This fact does not reduce the critical nature of expertise under uncertainty (Zsambok and Klein 1996). The notion of uncertainty in expert literature is related to novelty creation (Ericsson et al. 1993; Ericsson and Smith 1991), high velocity of environmental change, and dynamic problem solving (Read et al. 2003). Research suggests that in time-critical and less structured [1] fields such as medicine and fire fighting, skilled expert performers produce superior actions when compared with their less skilled peers, even in situations where the individuals had no prior experience (Ericsson and Lehmann 1996). Under such conditions, organization and reasoning drive quick response without requiring justification for the solution (Patel et al. 1996). Therefore, we suggest that expertise in the VC industry could be accumulated in a way that is similar to how medical expertise is acquired and used in the face of uncertain diagnostic and emergency situations (Read et al. 2003). Such attributes (i.e. time-critical and lack of structure) seem highly applicable in the entrepreneurial environment. Empirical evidence of this exists in the case of VC decision making, wherein Shepherd, Zacharakis et al. (2003) explored Shanteau's (1992) ten attributes of tasks that allowed predictions as to whether expertise would improve or impair decision-making performance. Their findings suggest that growing expertise on the part of VC's should, in fact, lead to increments in their performance.

Further, the literature on expertise suggests that experts in a given task requiring decision-making, may show higher judgment accuracy (Dreyfuss and Dreyfuss 1986; Nosofsky 1986) and as a result, VCs may choose the "right" company more accurately as experience increases (Shepherd et al. 2003). However Rabin (1998) suggests that experts might be susceptible to inferring *too much from too little* information and misreading evidence. This puts experts at a particular risk because, as part of their acquisition of expertise, they may have become so mechanical that they *miss things*. These conditions worsen when the decision maker is placed in an environment characterized by high uncertainty, ambiguity, and incomplete and asymmetric information – characteristics of the environments VCs operate in. This may lead to ascribing inappropriate weight to information cues and to making errors combining them (Camerer et al. 1991). Therefore, the decision environment poses significant challenges to understanding and analyzing decision criteria used by VCs in decision making. Researchers in expert systems literature suggest that while the decision process may be fraught with processes of random or systematic errors, understanding the nature and relationships among attributes for decision making is important. The following section addresses these shortcomings in the context of current approaches to understanding VC decision making, and explains how latent decision structures may provide more reliable and valid understanding of the VC decision process.

3. PREVIOUS RESEARCH ON THE VC DECISION PROCESS

In order to explore the drawbacks with previous research, it is necessary to understand the VC decision making process. In brief, a typical business plan goes through two stages in the decision making process – screening and due diligence (Sahlman 1990; Tyebjee et al. 1984). In the screening process, VCs evaluate whether a business plan deserves further interest. According to Sahlman (1990), almost 80 percent of the business plans are rejected in the screening process. Business plans that merit further attention undergo the due diligence process, during which venture characteristics are further scrutinized and venture team potential is judged. Often, VCs invest in syndicates and therefore make use of multiple due diligence processes. Additionally, prior research ignores the underlying heterogeneity among decision makers and assumes similar decision making challenges.

Research thus far suggests that conditions of VC decision making are neither structured nor unambiguous, and that the knowledge elicitation process and the eventual representation process pose significant challenges under conditions of VC decision making, due to the nature of available information, biases, and heterogeneity in decision making (Shepherd 1999; Zacharakis et al. 1998). The literature on expertise suggests that elicitation and aggregation techniques are factors for explaining a set of key investment parameters. This literature also suggests that knowledge acquisition and its representation from experts requires developing an understanding of the decision making process (Cooke and McDonald 1987).

Each of these is discussed in detail in light of previous studies. Specifically, the roles of interviewing and verbal protocol techniques in eliciting knowledge are discussed using a researcher-specified list of attributes or scenarios. It is suggested that techniques such as these may compromise knowledge elicitation either through the nature of tacit decision making or through researcher-defined decision criteria. Additionally, the knowledge representation approaches typically imposed by researchers are assessed. These knowledge representation approaches entail the use of empirical approaches that make assumptions about the knowledge representation which do not mesh with actual decision making. While prior research has discussed limitations of espoused criteria and verbal protocols (Franke et al. 2006), this study specifically focuses on widely used additive utility models (for example conjoint analysis) that makes assumptions that do not lend readily to VC decision making.

3.1. Knowledge Elicitation

The key hurdle in knowledge elicitation under VC decision making is that of necessity of introspection and verbal expression of tacit knowledge and decision processes. Worse yet, with increasing expertise, such elicitation is increasingly difficult (Johnson 1988). Prior research aimed at eliciting knowledge structures of VCs typically made use of a list of attributes that researchers suggest VCs utilize when investing in a particular venture. Such operationalizations have been typically analyzed using verbal protocols (Sandberg et al. 1988), ranking methods (Macmillan et al. 1985; Macmillan et al. 1987; Tyebjee et al. 1984), and in the last decade by using additive utility methods (Shepherd 1999; Shepherd and Zacharakis 1999; Shepherd et al. 1998; Shepherd et al. 2003; Zacharakis et al. 1998; Zacharakis and Meyer 2000; Zacharakis and Shepherd 2001).

The problem with using ranking methods and verbal protocols in knowledge elicitation is that introspection and verbal expression of knowledge are difficult tasks for experts. Additionally, research on the subject suggests that an expert's ability to express knowledge is inversely related to their experience (Johnson 1988). Experts may not accurately report mental states or mental processes through introspections (Cooke 1994, 1999; Hoffman et al. 1995). This is why when asked to provide explanations for their behavior, experts often produce reasons, rules, or strategies that do not correspond to their actual behavior (Rowe et al. 1996). Additionally, expert knowledge consists of automatic or compiled mental processes. Therefore, processes or strategies used by experts might not be available for introspection (Johnson 1967; Jonassen et al. 1993; Schvaneveldt et al. 1985; Shepard 1962a, 1962b; Shiffrin and Schneider 1977).

Further, Cooke and McDonald (1987) contend that even if experts could accurately *introspect* their decision process, they still face the problem of transferring that knowledge to the researcher as well as dealing with the subjective interpretation of the researcher. Typically a researcher is alien to a VC's domain and the VC is alien to the knowledge representation processes. The VC's decision process is observed or recorded, interpreted, transformed, and then analyzed through the researcher's analytical framework, making the representation of knowledge an artifact of the researcher's framework. In addition, VCs may not be able toexpress the mental processes while explaining the investment decision process to researchers.

3.2. Knowledge Representation

Literature suggests that expert knowledge consists of concepts, relations, features, chunks, plans, heuristics, theories, mental models, etc. However, one must find the means to create a closer representation so as to reduce mismatches. Cooke and McDonald (1987) suggest that "to avoid such a mismatch... knowledge representation of the system should be driven by a formal knowledge acquisition process which would reveal the contents and organization of expert knowledge." Typically, researchers analyzing elicited data impose theoretical or empirical constraints with regard to how knowledge is represented.

A researcher may impose theoretically borrowed relations that are empirically implemented. For example, empirical models may justify independent effects of the competitive environment, market, and teams, whereas VCs may not see the relationships in a similar vein. Irrespective of the approach, the goal must be to match an expert's knowledge representation with the analytical framework (Camerer et al. 1991). Additionally, experts differ considerably from novices' reasoning and knowledge structure. Imposing structures and processes based on general knowledge is inconsistent with highly knowledge-specific and tacit approaches used by VCs. This strongly suggests that the use of researcher-defined criteria in eliciting or imposing decision criteria is insufficient and inadequate.

Therefore, while literature has pointed out drawbacks of espoused criteria, verbal protocols, and cognitive biases (Franke et al. 2006; Shepherd et al. 2003), the currently accepted knowledge representation approach from additive utility models has limited application in understanding VC decision making. The key issue with applicability of conjoint analysis is the requirement of independence of attributes to implement assessment of independent scenarios (Green et al. 2001). However, the limitations of applicability of conjoint analysis are discussed in detail below.

First, one of the key assumptions of the technique is the addition of part worth utilities (Green et al. 2001). This assumes the inherent independence of attributes. Typically, in marketing, conjoint models are associated with products whose attributes are sharply distinct and hence uncorrelated (Green et al. 2001). In other words, changing the level of one attribute does not affect the level of other attributes. This is a strong assumption in the context of ventures, where much of the potential of a venture is endogenously determined. A better opportunity may result in a better competitive positioning and market potential, which in turn is highly correlated to better venture teams. Thus, the attributes of a business plan. Therefore, such dependence of utilities may not be strictly additive and may result in unstable estimates and poor predictions (Green et al. 2001; Huber et al. 1993). More important, scenarios presented to a decision maker in a conjoint experiment may not be assumed to be independent of the other scenarios.

Second, the greater the number of attributes to be assessed, the higher the cognitive load required on the part of decision makers. Additive utility models (e.g. conjoint analysis) require VCs to fill in for missing information for a given scenario. As in verbal protocol models, decision making is explored under hypothetical conditions (Shepherd 1999). While a researcher may eliminate redundant or nonsensical scenarios, the accuracy of judgments on the part of the decision maker is an artifact of a list of attributes developed by the researcher.

Third, these scenarios pose another problem in the way they are presented. They cause the participants to lose sight of the forest for the trees, to borrow from an old cliché. In other words, independent assessments of scenarios may result in overrating of certain features that may not be important to the overall picture. For example, analyzing scenarios based on market and team, and competitive advantage and team, may not result in similar assessments. Additionally, choice variables such as "low" or "high" may have little value when the decision maker does not focus on the complete business plan. In reality, VCs make decisions of investing with the complete business plan in mind, and not focusing on individual parts. More important, under conditions of uncertainty and ambiguity, decision processes may be highly inconsistent, intransitive, and simply ambiguous (Zsambok et al. 1996). Therefore, decision making scenarios without complete business plans, assessed under high uncertainty, may result in reduced validity of assessments of participants.

Finally, conjoint analysis does not put constraints on the shape of the utility function (Green et al. 2001; Green and Srinivasan 1990). While this may be a useful approach, typical scaling algorithms use a shape function that is less subject to random errors that could arise from the decision maker's perspective.

Other issues with using conjoint approaches in VC decision making are: (1) from a sociopsychological perspective, VCs do not take decision making as seriously under these conditions as they would when deciding on real investment decisions, and (2) as all VCs would prefer ventures with high market potential and experienced and capable teams, there could be a lack of reliability and validity in the VC judgment (Shanteau 1992; Tversky and Kahneman 1974). Additionally, research suggests that considering the structural aspect of utility as fully defined in an environment with limited information is unadvisable (Blaszczynski et al. 1997; Nakamura 1996; Parsons 1996; Pawlak 1999; Slowinski 1993; Slowinski and Stefanowski 1993, 1996).

These utility models could lead to the creation of cognitive biases that in turn increase the criticality of the stochastic component, which in turn could limit the provision of psychometric correction, beyond the obvious limitations of espoused criteria (Bishop and Heberlein 1990; Cameron and Huppert 1989; Diamond and Hausman 1994; Manski 2005; McFadden 1994, 1999). This suggests that most research to date has constrained the knowledge acquisition process by pre-selecting the knowledge representation process.

3.3. Formal Strategies for Knowledge Acquisition and Representation

Given the challenges with assumptions and implementations on the part of expert processes and analytical artifacts, literature on scaling techniques from cognitive psychology may be helpful, as it focuses on the information processing paradigm. More specifically, these methods focus on empirical findings in language, perception, memory, and problem solving to study representations of frames, scripts, features, propositions, and production systems (McFadden 1994). Psychological scaling algorithms empirically generate specific types of knowledge representations (e.g., spatial, hierarchical, network) (Cooke and McDonald, 1987). These techniques (specifically multidimensional/psychological scaling) combine elicitation and structuring aspects, and are more useful than traditional interview- or scenario-based knowledge elicitation techniques (Preston et al. 2005). They are also useful in the conceptual and refinement stages of the knowledge acquisition process. More important, research has found that scaling based elicitation techniques perform better than protocol analysis and interviewing (Burton et al. 1987), and addresses the typical drawbacks of conjoint analysis (Huber et al. 1993).

These psychological scaling techniques involve experts rating the similarity of different objects (usually chosen beforehand), followed by representing the rating as a distance on a scale, ranging from not similar to completely similar – the goal being the discovery of a rank order of objects within a problem domain. MDS developed by Kruskal (1977) is based on the use of the least squares method to fit the elicited data. Therefore while conjoint experiments may help elicit knowledge and the relative importance of espoused criteria, the researcher substitutes aggregation statistically because the nature of the combination of scenarios increases exponentially.

Additionally, MDS does not make any distributional assumptions about the underlying data, and given the heterogeneous nature of decision making and knowledge structures of the VCs, this is very important. Also, traditional techniques based on statistical representation are inherently unstable and the representations of knowledge may change with assumptions and processes of underlying technique. Finally, MDS provides an intuitive understanding to the practitioners without substituting their intuitions with the findings.

4. METHODOLOGY

The analysis was conducted in three steps. First, a set of attributes, as well as what they meant to the VCs, was identified using an adapted version of free-listing and focus group sessions. Second, using the identified attributes, a group of experts were asked to evaluate a set of business plans (all of which were either funded or rejected by VCs). These industry experts evaluated the business plans based on an understanding of common meanings of business plan attributes provided to them. Industry experts were used, as they could provide a more objective assessment than asking VCs to re-evaluate their investments, which could lead to retrospective and attribution biases. The experts were not aware of which plans were funded and which were not funded by the VCs. Third, based on the evaluations by the experts, MDS was used to identify knowledge structures, followed by PRO-FIT and QDA to validate the key dimensions identified through MDS. To further ensure that our analysis was not an artifact of the parametric methods, AUTOCLASS (Bayesian mixture models) was used.

5. DATA

The sample originally consisted of 200 business plans obtained from VCs, of which 72 were funded and 128 were not funded. In order to improve generalizability and understanding of common latent structures across VCs in the US, business plans were obtained from VC firms on the east and west coasts of the US. Further, to reduce heterogeneity across industries, only business plans from firms in the high tech industry who were seeking start-up funding during the year 2004 were considered. Given the fact that the experts are aware of the high rates of rejection of business plans, they could randomly not fund a large number of business plans and still make statistically correct predictions. Therefore in order to increase the reliability of the study, 72 of the 128 non funded business plans were randomly chosen. Evenly distributing the business plans enabled the elimination of chance predictions by the experts.[2] Therefore, the final dataset consisted of 144 business plans, of which 72 were funded and 72 were not funded by VCs. To ensure that decision processes were independent, only business plans that VCs had invested in as individuals, as opposed to investment via syndication, were considered.

Data concerning the attributes used by VCs were collected by way of an adapted version of free-listing using 58 participants, who included VCs, angel investors, and commercial lenders, and two focus group sessions using 12 VCs and 15 VCs, respectively, from metropolitans areas in the midwestern United States. The free-listing and focus group part of our study is described below.

5.1. Identifying Common Meanings

The first step was to identify criteria that VCs use in making funding decisions. Towards this end, data were gathered from VCs, angel investors, and commercial lenders. The individuals were approached at a venture club meeting at a midwestern US city, and asked to participate. A modified form of the free-listing data collection technique was used, wherein respondents were asked a question about a particular domain and were invited to respond with a list of answers that represent pertinent elements in that domain (Weller and Romney 1988). Free-listing is recommended when little is known about a domain because it allows participants to provide information without researcher bias (Weller et al. 1988). The free-listing technique presents problems if different individuals have different definitions for the same term, or if different respondents use the same term, but have different meanings. To avoid this problem, 22 criteria were identified that prior literature in strategy, finance, and sociology found to play an important role in the success of business ventures, as well as criteria suggested by the popular press. Examples of criteria included potential market share (Schmalensee 1981), revolutionary nature of product/service (Aaker and Day 1986; Williamson 1985), use of technology (Aaker et al. 1986), timing of the new venture (Aaker et al. 1986; Mitchell 1991), competitive advantage (Robinson and Fornell 1985; Schmalensee 1981), value added by the product/service (Andrews 1987; Shepherd 1999), ability to attract and retain customers (Robinson et al. 1985; Schmalensee 1981), soundness of business model (Chatterjee 1998), ability to protect intellectual property (Golder and Tellis 1993), product life (Golder et al. 1993), communication skills, clear and realistic funding needs, potential for profitability, networks/contacts, potential for growth, flexibility (willingness to change), and management experience (Hannan and Freeman 1989; Stinchcombe 1965).

This list of terms with definitions for each term was distributed to the 120 participants, who were asked to identify the criteria they used to determine whether they would invest in a new business. Fifty-eight responses were received. Generally, 20 to 30 respondents are recommended to get a complete picture using the free-listing technique (Weller et al. 1988). Respondents were also asked to list any criteria that were not part of the list provided to them and explain what they meant by any added criteria, and to rank the criteria in their lists in terms of their importance. Six new criteria were added by respondents, giving us a total of 28 criteria. From the 28 criteria provided by the participants and their rankings, seven criteria were eliminated because they appeared on few lists and were ranked very low. This gave rise to a list of 21 criteria.

This set of 21 criteria was presented to a focus group of 12 individuals that included venture capitalists and angel investors (both institutional and private) from a midwestern US city. These 12 individuals were contacted through the researchers' personal contacts and asked to participate in the study. Cumulatively, the participants in this group were the lead investors in over fifty different businesses. The purpose of this focus group was to 1) determine whether the terms and definitions used earlier were consistent, 2) weight the different criteria in terms of their importance in funding decisions, 3) identify scales that should be used to evaluate each criterion, and 4) group the 21 criteria into meaningful categories.

Finally, the categories and the criteria within each category, along with the definitions for each criterion, were presented to another focus group of 15 VCs from a different midwestern US city. These individuals were also contacted through the researchers' personal contacts and asked to participate in the study. This group was used to validate/change the criteria and scales, and to determine how important each category was in their funding decisions. The data gathered in this stage, together with the data gathered from the previous focus group, were used to weight the different criteria that are important in the VC decision-making process.

5.2. Expert Evaluation

The purpose of this stage was to determine how well each of the plans did on the criteria identified in the first stage. Towards this end, nine experts were asked to evaluate the business plans. The experts were individuals from a midwestern city in the US. On average, they had 18 years of experience in dealing with VC funding in the high tech sector. Each of the 72 funded business plans was evaluated three times, and 71[3] of the unfunded business plans were evaluated three times. As one of the unfunded business plans did not receive three evaluations, it was taken out of the analysis, leaving us with 72 funded business plans and 71 unfunded business plans. Each expert evaluated an average of two plans per week over a 23-week period in 2005 using the criteria established in the first stage.[4] In addition to rating each plan on the established criteria, each expert was asked to indicate whether a plan should be funded. After expert evaluation, seven out of these 21 criteria were removed from the analysis as they pertained to presentation quality of the business plan, types of financial documentation, and funding milestones. The final set of criteria are startup experience, industry experience, leadership experience, management experience, market size, customer adoption, revenue generated, entry timing, competition, technological advantage, strategy, intellectual property rights, value added, and profit margins.

6. ANALYTICAL APPROACH

A synopsis of the data analysis approach can be seen in figure 1 below. Given the nature and structure of decision making, a latent structure confirmed by multidimensional scaling (MDS) and AUTOCLASS was developed. Both of these techniques do not make assumptions about the underlying distribution of the data.[5] First, the nature of underlying attributes for a given venture using MDS was identified. To create confirmatory and more deductive inferences from the identified structure, the linear PRO-FIT and nonlinear QDA techniques were used to identify relative importance of attributes identified through MDS. Finally, even though MDS and PRO-FIT explain substantial variance, there is a possibility that heterogeneity[6] exists among the VCs latent structure in preferences when it comes to funding plans, but as these inferences are based on parametric methods, it is likely that VCs who depend on their ability to manage market and agency risk would pick business plans accordingly. This is where the Bayesian unsupervised model, AUTOCLASS, comes into play, as it may help address some possible shortcomings of parametric approaches, and further enhance methodological convergence and inference validity. AUTOCLASS models the data as a mixture of conditionally independent classes. Advantages of using Bayesian unsupervised models include: (1) they are parameter-free, (2) user input is not required, (3) prior distributions of the model offer a theoretically justifiable method for affecting the model construction, (4) these models work with probabilities and can hence be expected to produce smooth and robust visualizations with discrete data containing nominal and ordinal attributes and (5) the Bayesian approach has no limit for minimum sample size (Kontkanen et al., 2000). A quick overview of the analysis is presented in Figure 1 below, starting with parametric methods.

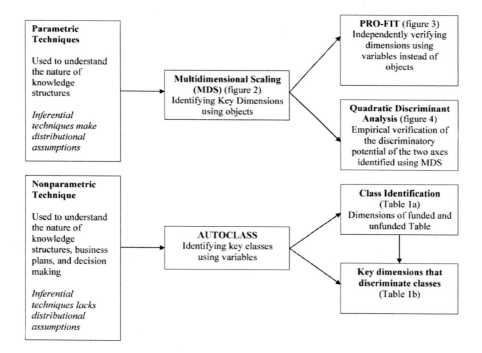

Figure 1. Analytical Techniques.

7. RESULTS

Furthermore, adequate power was found with the proposed techniques. For two dimensions identified with MDS, the sample size falls within recommendations from Carroll and Arabie (1980). Also, as mentioned earlier, high levels of reliability across experts in discriminating funded and nonfunded business plans indicates high effect sizes of the set of attributes. Thus, considering average effect size of 0.5 and $\alpha=0.05$, with a sample size of 143, power is substantially high ($\beta>0.9$). Furthermore, such high power means that results of nonlinear discriminant analysis will be more reliable. Similarly, for unsupervised Bayesian classification, the minimal sample size issue is not critical (Kontkanen et al. 2000a; Kontkanen et al. 2000b). However, sizes of 58 and 143 are more than adequate (Raudys and Jain 1991).

The degree of agreement among experts' business plan evaluations was assessed, and the inter-rater reliability among experts using attributes identified by VCs on funded and unfunded business plans was 0.93, suggesting high inter-rater reliability. Additionally, the difference between funded and nonfunded business plans based on expert ratings was significant ($p<0.015$). Logistic regression using expert ratings explained 89 percent of the variance between funded and nonfunded business plans. To further confirm the degree of matching between experts and actual decisions, a composite score was created using principal component analysis. The reliability for expert loadings was 0.94.

The first decision in MDS is the choice of number of dimensions that capture the underlying latent structure. A typical statistical program gives a range between one and six. However, choosing a number in between the range provided by the software is ad hoc, and certain important dimensions could be missed, if more than six dimensions are required. In this case, the similarity matrix was first subject to principal components analysis (PCA). The first three components accounted for 94.78 percent of the variance – the first component 54.71 percent, the second component 33.54 percent, and the third component 6.53 percent. Thus, three dimensions would be sufficient to describe the data. Based on previous studies and as recommended by Kruskal and Wish (1978), Young's stress formula was used, and the stress was found to be least (stress = 0.061) for two dimensions. Additionally, the reduction in stress with increased dimensions is minimal. Furthermore, the minimal variation identified by the third component of the PCA supports the inference that two dimensions are adequate to represent the decision structure.

Figure 2 below shows the spatial distribution of funded and nonfunded business plans. The fact that the funded business plans fall toward the left side of the graph suggests that the first dimension is an important indicator in signifying funding criteria. Based on Ohlson (1980), two logit analyses were considered as the ability of dimensions to differentiate between funded and nonfunded business plans. First a traditional logit was considered, with dependent variable as funded (1) and nonfunded (0) business plans. Based on this analysis, the first two dimensions were found to be significant at the 0.95 level. This mapping also suggests that two dimensions are sufficient for appropriate representations.

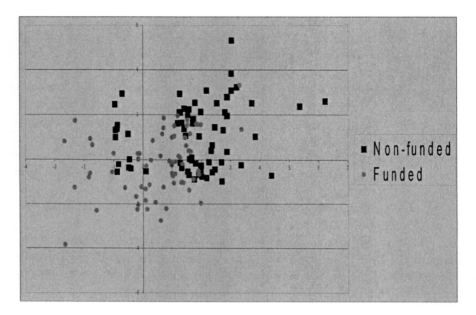

Figure 2. MDS Analysis.

MDS analysis focused on the creation of a map wherein it can be seen that funded business plans differ from nonfunded business plans. Understanding the results above, however, requires the use of PROFIT[7]. PRO-FIT is a regression-based technique that explains the degree to which a given level of an attribute is associated with a business plan. The results are represented graphically in Figure 3 below. Due to space restrictions, all the diagnostic statistics are not reported. Most of the cases had an R^2 greater than 0.9. For each of the 14 attributes used, a line is drawn through the space such that the value of the attribute increases with direction of the line. The attributes that load on the horizontal axis shows that dimension one is associated with the competitive environment (the horizontal axis), and the attributes that load on the vertical axis show that the second dimension is associated with the characteristics of the founding team (the vertical axis). These lines indicate that the competitive environment is the most important indicator of funding and nonfunding decisions.

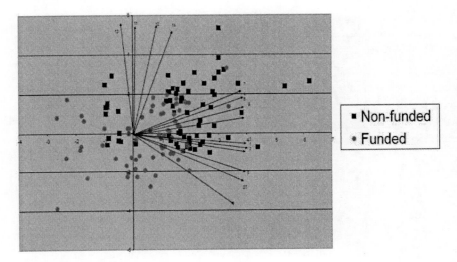

Figure 3. PRO-FIT Analysis.

Next, as suggested by Richardson and Davidson (1984), there may be a statistical inference problem if the variance-covariance matrices are different. While this is more applicable in discriminant analysis, in the case of logit analysis, nonlinear terms must be included in the analysis (Mar-Molinero and Ezzamel 1991; Mar-Molinero 1988). Using a general linear model, a saturated model with quadratic and interaction terms was used and later simplified using standard procedures outlined by Dobson (2002). It was inferred that the square of the second coordinate was a necessary dimension to capture richness of the data. Therefore, probabilities for funding could be calculated, while other points in the space are occupied by hypothetical business plans (Mar-Molinero et al. 1991), and every point in the space could be allocated a probability of funding. Points in the space with the same probability of funding could be joined to create an *iso-nonfunding* surface. This suggests that even though there is no simple discriminating frontier between funded and nonfunded business plans, one may use a set of discriminating frontiers with different probabilities. Therefore using a set ranging from 1.0 to 0.25 in the increments of 0.25, the 0.5 iso-line is the discriminant.[8] This model (the best discriminatory model) misclassifies only 9 business plans out of 143 (four funded and five unfunded business plans were misclassified; misclassification rate of 6.3 percent). This can be seen in figure 4 below, wherein the 0.5 curve correctly classifies 93.7 percent of the business plans.

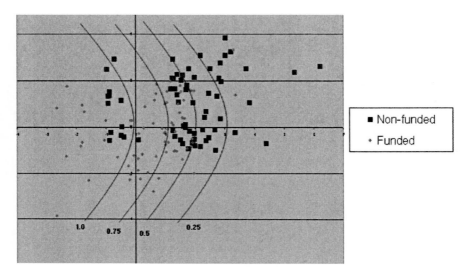

Figure 4. Quadratic Discriminant Analysis.

Therefore, based on QDA and PRO-FIT, it can be inferred that there are two key dimensions – competitive environment and founding team. However, the nonlinear nature of the founding team suggests that venture team characteristics are important to a certain extent, after which this effect declines. Thus, having a better team has decreasing returns. Finally, the degree of heterogeneity in VC funding is assessed using a distribution-free inference technique, AUTOCLASS,[9] which requires no class imposition on the part of the researcher.

As seen in Table 1(a) below, AUTOCLASS also indicates that two distinct clusters exist. The class weight of 77 unfunded and 66 funded is very close to the original 71 unfunded and 72 funded. Therefore, heterogeneity is assessed for funded and nonfunded business plans. The results in Table 1(b) show 12 of the 14 criteria important for differentiating the two groups. More important, results from table 1(b) suggest that management team, industry experience, startup experience, value added, market size, competition, timing, technology, IP, harvest potential, leadership/CEO experience, and strategy (listed in their order of importance) are criteria utilized by VCs when not funding a business plan. High class strength (Cheeseman and Stutz 1996) suggests that there is negligible heterogeneity among VC firms in funding and nonfunding. Therefore, factors leading to heterogeneity are not explored.

Table 1. AUTOCLASS Results

Table 1(a) Class Strength10

Class #	Log of class strength	Relative Class Strength	Class Wt.	Normalized Class weight
0	-42.1	1.00	77	0.54
1	-50.3	0.67	66	0.46
(real distribution is: 72 funded + 71 not funded)				

Table 1(b): Within class attribute measures

Attribute	I-jk 11	Attribute	I-jk
Group 0 (nonfunded business		Group 1 (funded business plans)	
Management Experience	2.31	Value Added	3.01
Industry Experience	2.16	Market Size	2.97
Startup Experience	2.11	Competition	2.71
Value Added	2.08	Entry Timing	2.57
Market Size	2.05	Technology	2.40
Competition	2.01	Technological advantage	2.36
Entry Timing	1.98	Strategy	2.25
Technological advantage	1.76	Startup Experience	1.88
Intellectual Property Rights	1.47	Industry Experience	1.76
Harvest Potential	1.21	Leadership Experience	1.69
Leadership Experience	1.07	Management Experience	1.67
Strategy	1.04	Harvest Potential	1.32
Class entropy with respect to global entropy	8.47		9.23

8. DISCUSSION AND IMPLICATIONS

First, contrary to previous studies on VC investment decisions that focused mainly on espoused criteria, this study focuses on funding criteria, trying to replicate latent investment preferences of VCs (using real business plans), and provides a more contingent view to the VC investment decision process. The findings explain the prior research in terms of the importance of a team and go further by explaining that VCs use the competitive environment more intensely, while the venture team, though important, is of limited help beyond a certain extent. This suggests that team composition is a major factor in explaining why a business plan gets rejected, but is not significant in explaining why a business plan gets funded. This finding therefore contrasts with most prior studies, which identify venture team as the key funding criteria, and goes against the popular notion that suggests that an *A team and B opportunity beats a B team and an A opportunity*. The findings also suggest that teams have a decreasing return to scale. Previous research regarding the relationship between characteristics of the founding team and team effectiveness is inconsistent and inconclusive (Norburn 1986; Norburn and Birley 1988; O'Reilly et al. 1993). These findings lead Priem (1990) to propose a curvilinear relationship between the characteristics of the top management team and venture performance (Pettigrew 1992). Shepherd (1999) found that VCs' assessment policies of new venture survival were in fact consistent with those that literature suggested would increase the survival chances of the firm. Therefore, even though the findings are surprising, they are exactly in line with what Priem (1990) had proposed as to the curvilinear relationship between team composition and the VC investment decision.

Second, by presenting alternative methodologies to understand the latent structure of VC knowledge structure, the current study provides alternative approaches for future researchers who wish to study repeat entrepreneurs. In contexts where it is difficult to explicitly explain the thought and decision processes (e.g. entrepreneurial contexts), using MDS in conjunction with other confirmatory practices may be useful in eliciting knowledge and decision structures. Understanding such knowledge structures has great implications for pedagogy and entrepreneurs alike. Also, the homogeneity in the process of decision making may indicate the syndication effect on VC decision making. An increased number of investments made in syndicates, and high levels of network associated with creating value in investments, may result in substantial development of a common outlook. This is substantiated by the high levels of homogeneity in VC decision making for funded and nonfunded ventures.

Finally, from a practical standpoint, entrepreneurs face substantial constraints in obtaining finance and therefore understanding specific investment criteria is of paramount importance. Understanding criteria for funding may substantially improve their odds of funding. Based on the findings in this paper, entrepreneurs need not only to assemble an effective team, but also need to clearly demonstrate the venture potential of their business venture. From a pedagogical point of view, teachers can help students (potential entrepreneurs) understand fundamental VC decision criteria, and show them how matching their characteristics with VC investment criteria could assist them in their efforts of obtaining financing for their ventures. These findings present a specific challenge to pedagogy in terms of long-held beliefs about the importance of venture teams. Therefore, for teachers an increased challenge is to teach students how to correctly identify and position ventures to reflect the future potential of the venture.

9. LIMITATIONS

Like any study, this one is not without its limitations. First, even though evaluations by experts demonstrated high reliability, the investment process undertaken by VCs is complex and drawn out. Thorough due diligence and interactions between VCs and teams are not considered. However, focusing on the final decisions may help shunt the decision process, because outsiders cannot control or affect the decision process. Thus, focusing on key criteria that lead to investment may be more useful to entrepreneurs. Secondly, although the analytical framework helps provide convergence, the data come from a narrow time frame from one industry. Thus the generalizability of the findings may be limited. However, given the changing knowledge structures over time, not only the nature attributes, but the relative weights may also change. Therefore, to remove the effects of heterogeneity over time and across VCs, a narrow time frame of data is necessary.

Finally, because the entire investment process was not closely monitored, the issue of equifinality in decision making may be at play. In other words, VCs may have reached the same decisions through many different criteria and attributes. Thus, identified criteria from one group of VCs may not be applicable to others. This was partially controlled for by using a set of multiple statistical techniques with a different set of assumptions. Similarly, the high discriminatory power of expert assessment with VC investment decision explains why the set of attributes may actually be relevant in decision making.

Overall, based on all the analyses, it can be inferred that (1) venture potential is a better indicator of funding than venture team; (2) while venture team has decreasing returns, it is a potential deal breaker for not getting funded; and (3) VCs have similar knowledge structures and preferences when it comes to funding and not funding actual business plans. In other words, VCs may be more willing to fund a marginal team with better venture potential than a good team with limited venture potential.

10. CONCLUSION

Using a framework for expert knowledge structures, a set of attributes most critical to VC investment decision making were identified. The paper adds to the current literature by deriving a set of attributes that are widely accepted in the VC decision-making process, rather than provide vague attributes such as market potential. The results suggest that market factors are most important in determining whether a business does receive VC funding, and the quality of the management team is most important in determining whether a business does not receive funding. More important, compared with previous research it provides a more contingent view to the VC investment decision process. Even though the venture team ability is a minimum requirement and a venture may not get funded if the team is not qualified, this qualification is a prerequisite for considering venture potential. VCs are willing to accept a marginal team if the venture potential is high, but the prime reason for not funding is the lack of an appropriate team.

REFERENCES

Aaker, D. A., Day, G. S. 1986. The perils of high growth markets. *Strategic Management Journal*, 7: 409- 421.

Andrews, K. R. 1987. *The Concept of Corporate Strategy*. Homewood, IL: Irwin.

Bishop, R. C., Heberlein, T. A. 1990. The Contingent Valuation Method. In R. L. Johnson,G. V. Johnson (Eds.), *Economic Valuation of Natural Resources: Issues, Theory, and Applications*. Boulder, CO: Westview Press.

Blaszczynski, J., Greco, S., Slowinski, R. 1997. Multi-criteria classification - A new scheme for application of dominance-based decision rules. *European Journal of Operational Research*, 181(3): 1030-1044. Borgatti, S. P. 1996. ANTHROPAC 4.98X. Analytic Technologies.

Borgatti, S. P. 1998. Elicitation Techniques for Cultural Domain Analysis. In J. J. Schensul, M. D. LeCompte,B. K. Nastasi,S. P. Borgatti (Eds.), *Enhanced Ethnographic Methods: Audiovisual Techniques, Focused Group Interviews, and Elicitation Techniques*: 115–151: AltaMira Press.

Burton, A. M., Shadbolt, N. R., Hedgecock, A. P., Rugg, G., Moralee, D. S. 1987. *Research and Development in Expert Systems IV:* Cambridge University Press, Cambridge.

Camerer, C. F., Johnson, E. J. 1991. The process-performance paradox in expert judgment: How can experts know so much and predict so badly. *Toward a general theory of expertise: Prospects and limits*: 195–217.

Cameron, T. A., Huppert, D. D. 1989. OLS versus ML estimation of nonmarket resource values with payment card interval data. *Journal of Environmental Economics and Management*, 17(3): 230-246.

Carroll, J. D., Chang, J. J. 1969. A general index of nonlinear correlation and its application to the problem of relating physical and psychological dimensions. *Unpublished manuscript, Bell Telephone Laboratories*.

Carroll, J. D., Arabie, P. 1980. Multidimensional Scaling. *Annual Review of Psychology*, 31(1): 607-649. Chatterjee, S. 1998. Delivering desired outcomes efficiently: The creative key to competitive strategy. *California Management Review*, 40(2): 4-95.

Cheeseman, P., Stutz, J. 1996. Bayesian classification (AutoClass): Theory and results. *Advances in Knowledge Discovery and Data Mining*, 180.

Cooke, N. J. 1994. Varieties of knowledge elicitation techniques. *International Journal of Human-Computer Studies*, 41(6): 801-849.

Cooke, N. J. 1999. Knowledge elicitation. In F. T. Durso,R. S. Nickerson,R. W. Schvaneveldt,S. T. Dumais,D. S. Lindsay,M. T. H. Chi (Eds.), *Handbook of Applied Cognition*: 479–509. Chichester: John Wiley.

Cooke, N. M., McDonald, J. E. 1987. The application of psychological scaling techniques to knowledge elicitation for knowledge-based systems. *International Journal of Man-Machine Studies*, 26(4): 533- 550.

Diamond, P. A., Hausman, J. A. 1994. Contingent Valuation: Is Some Number better than No Number? *The Journal of Economic Perspectives*, 8(4): 45-64.

Dobson, A. J. 2002. An Introduction to Generalised Linear Models.

Dreyfuss, H., Dreyfuss, S. 1986. Mind over machine. The power of human intuition and expertise in the era of the computer: New York, NY: The Free Press.

Dubini, P. 1989. The influence of motivations and environment on business start-ups: Some hints for public policies. *Journal of Business Venturing*, 4(1): 11-26.

Ericsson, K. A., Smith, J. 1991. Prospects and limits ofthe empirical study of expertise: an introduction. In A. Ericsson,J. Smith (Eds.), *Toward a general theory of expertise: Prospects and Limits*: 344. New York: Cambridge University Press.

Ericsson, K. A., Krampe, R. T., Tesch-Romer, C. 1993. The role of deliberate practice in the acquisition of expert performance. *Psychological Review*, 100(3): 363-406.

Ericsson, K. A., Lehmann, A. C. 1996. EXPERT AND EXCEPTIONAL PERFORMANCE: Evidence of Maximal Adaptation to Task Constraints. *Annual Review of Psychology*, 47(1): 273-305.

Franke, N., Gruber, M., Harhoff, D., Henkel, J. 2006. What you are is what you like--similarity biases in venture capitalists' evaluations of start-up teams. *Journal of Business Venturing*, 21(6): 802-826.

Golder, P. N., Tellis, G. J. 1993. Pioneer advantage: marketing logic or marketing legend? *Journal of Marketing Research*, 30: 158-170.

Green, P. E., Srinivasan, V. 1990. Conjoint Analysis in Marketing: New Developments with Implications for Research and Practice. *Journal of Marketing*, 54(4): 3-19.

Green, P. E., Krieger, A. M., Wind, Y. 2001. Thirty Years of Conjoint Analysis: Reflections and Prospects. *Interfaces*, 31(4): 56-73.

Hall, J., Hofer, C. W. 1993. Venture capitalists' decision criteria in new venture evaluation. *Journal of Business Venturing*, 8(1): 25-42.

Hannan, M. T., Freeman, J. 1989. *Organizational Ecology*. Cambridge, MA.: Harvard University Press. Hoffman, R. R., Shadbolt, N. R., Burton, A. M., Klein, G. 1995. Eliciting knowledge from experts: a methodological analysis. *Organizational behavior and human decision processes(Print)*, 62(2): 129-158.

Huber, J., Wittink, D. R., Fiedler, J. A., Miller, R. 1993. The Effectiveness of Alternative Preference Elicitation Procedures in Predicting Choice. *Journal of Marketing Research*, 30(1): 105-114.

Johnson, E. J. 1988. Expertise and decisions under uncertainty: Performance and process. In M. L. H. Chi,R.

Glaser,M. J. Farr (Eds.), *The nature of expertise*: 209-228. Hillsdale, NJ: Erlbaum.

Johnson, S. C. 1967. Hierarchical clustering schemes. *Psychometrika*, 32(3): 241-254.

Jonassen, D. H., Beissner, K., Yacci, M. 1993. *Structural Knowledge CL: Techniques for Representing, Conveying, and Acquiring Structural Knowledge*. Hillsdale, NJ: Erlbaum.

Kontkanen, P., Lahtinen, J., Myllymaki, P., Silander, T., Tirri, H. 2000a. Using Bayesian networks for visualizing highdimensional data. *Intelligent Data Analysis*.

Kontkanen, P., Myllymäki, P., Silander, T., Tirri, H., Grünwald, P. 2000b. On predictive distributions and Bayesian networks. *Statistics and Computing*, 10(1): 39-54.

Kruskal, J. B. 1977. Multidimensional scaling and other methods for discovering structure. In Enslein.,D. A. Ralston,Wilf. (Eds.), *Statistical Methods for Digital Computers*, Vol. 3: 296-339. New York: Wiley Kruskal, J. B., Wish, M. 1978. *Multidimensional Scaling*. London: Sage.

Macmillan, I. C., Siegel, R., Narasimha, P. N. S. 1985. Criteria used by venture capitalists to evaluate new venture proposals. *Journal of Business Venturing*, 1(1): 119-128.

Macmillan, I. C., Zemann, L., Subbanarasimha, P. N. 1987. Criteria distinguishing successful from unsuccessful ventures in the venture screening process. *Journal of Business Venturing*, 2(2): 123- 137.

Manski, C. F. 2005. *Social Choice with Partial Knowledge of Treatment Response*: Princeton University Press.

Mar-Molinero, C., Ezzamel, M. 1991. Multidimensional scaling applied to company failure. *Omega*, 19: 259–274.

Mar-Molinero, C. M. 1988. Schools in Southampton: A Quantitative Approach to School Location, Closure and Staffing. *The Journal of the Operational Research Society*, 39(4): 339-350.

McFadden, D. 1994. Contingent Valuation and Social Choice. *American Journal of Agricultural Economics*, 76(4): 689-708.

McFadden, D. 1999. Rationality for Economists? *Journal of Risk and Uncertainty*, 19(1): 73-105.

Mitchell, W. 1991. Dual clocks: entry order influences on incumbent and newcomer market share and survival when specialized assets retain their value. *Strategic Management Journal*, 12: 85-100.

Nakamura, A. 1996. Rough logic based on incomplete information and its application. *International Journal of Approximate Reasoning*, 15(4): 367-378.

Norburn, D. 1986. GOGOs, YOYOs and DODOs: Company Directors and Industry Performance. *Strategic Management Journal*, 7(2): 101-117.

Norburn, D., Birley, S. 1988. The Top Management Team and Corporate Performance. *Strategic Management Journal*, 9(3): 225-237.

Nosofsky, R. M. 1986. Attention, similarity, and the identification-categorization relationship. *Journal of Experimental Psychology: General.*, 115(1): 39–57.

O'Reilly, C., Snyder, R., Boothe, J. 1993. Effects of executive team demography on organizational change. In G. Huber,W. Glick (Eds.), *Organizational change and redesign*: 147-175. New York: Oxford University Press.

Ohlson, J. A. 1980. Financial Ratios and the Probabilistic Prediction of Bankruptcy. *Journal of Accounting Research*, 18(1): 109-131.

Parsons, S. 1996. Current approaches to handling imperfect information in data and knowledge bases. *IEEE Transactions on Knowledge and Data Engineering*, 8(3): 353-372.

Patel, V. L., Kaufman, D. R., Magder, S. 1996. The acquisition of medical expertise in complex dynamic decision-making environments. In A. Ericsson (Ed.), *The road to excellence: The acquisition of expert performance in the arts and sciences, sports and games.*: 127-165. NJ: Erlbaum.: Hillsdale. Pawlak, Z. 1999. Rough classification. *International Journal of Human-Computer Studies*, 51(2): 369-383. Pettigrew, A. M. 1992. On Studying Managerial Elites. *Strategic Management Journal*, 13: 163-182.

Preston, S., Chapman, C., Pinfold, M., Smith, G. 2005. Knowledge acquisition for knowledge-based engineering systems. *International Journal of Information Technology and Management*, 4(1): 1-11. Priem, R. L. 1990. Top Management Team Group Factors, Consensus, and Firm Performance. *Strategic Management Journal*, 11(6): 469-478.

Rabin, M. 1998. Psychology and Economics. *Journal of Economic Literature*, 36(1): 11-46.

Raudys, S. J., Jain, A. K. 1991. Small sample size effects in statistical pattern recognition: recommendations for practitioners. *IEEE Transactions on Pattern Analysis and Machine Intelligence*, 13(3): 252-264.

Read, S., Wiltbank, R., Sarasvathy, S. D. 2003. What Do Entrepreneurs Really Learn From Experience? The Difference Between Expert and Novice Entrepreneurs. *BKERC Proceedings*.

Richardson, F. M., Davidson, L. F. 1984. On linear discrimination with accounting ratios. *Journal of Business Finance and Accounting*, 11(4): 511-525.

Robinson, W. T., Fornell, C. 1985. The sources of market pioneer advantages in consumer goods industries. *Journal of Marketing Research*, 222: 305-317.

Rowe, A. L., Cooke, N. J., Hall, E. P., Halgren, T. L. 1996. Toward an on-line knowledge assessment methodology: Building on the relationship between knowing and doing. *Journal of Experimental Psychology: Applied*, 2(1): 31-47.

Sahlman, W. 1990. The Structure and Governance of Venture-Capital Organizations. *Journal of Financial Economics*, 27(2): 473–521.

Sandberg, W. R., Schweiger, D. M., Hofer, C. W. 1988. The Use of Verbal Protocols in Determining Venture Capitalists' Decision Processes. *Entrepreneurship Theory and Practice*, 13(1): 8-20.

Schmalensee, R. 1981. Economies of scale and barriers to entry. *Journal of Political Economy*, 89: 1228-1238.

Schvaneveldt, R. W., Durso, F. T., Goldsmith, T. E., Breen, T. J., Cooke, N. M., Tucker, R. G., De Maio, J. C. 1985. Measuring the structure of expertise. *International Journal of Man-Machine Studies*, 23(6): 699-728.

Shanteau, J. 1992. Competence in experts: The role of task characteristics. *Organizational Behavior and Human Decision Processes*, 53(2): 252-266.

Shepard, R. N. 1962a. The analysis of proximities: Multidimensional scaling with an unknown distance function. I. *Psychometrika*, 27(2): 125-140.

Shepard, R. N. 1962b. The analysis of proximities: Multidimensional scaling with an unknown distance function. II. *Psychometrika*, 27(3): 219-246.

Shepherd, D. A. 1999. Venture Capitalists' Assessment of New Venture Survival. *Management Science*, 45(5): 621.

Shepherd, D. A., Zacharakis, A. 1999. Conjoint analysis: a new methodological approach for researching the decision policies of venture capitalists. *Venture Capital - An international journal of entrepreneurial finance*, 1(3): 197–217.

Shepherd, D. A., Zacharakis, A., Baron, R. A. 2003. VCs'Decision Processes: Evidence Suggesting More Experience may not Always be Better. *Journal of Business Venturing*, 18(3): 381-401.

Shiffrin, R. M., Schneider, W. 1977. Controlled and automatic human information processing: 11. Perceptual learning, automatic attending, and a general theory. *Psychological Review*, 84(2): 127-190.

Sinha, I., DeSarbo, W. S. 1998. An Integrated Approach toward the Spatial Modeling of Perceived Customer Value. *Journal of Marketing Research*, 35(2): 236-249.

Slowinski, R. 1993. Rough Set Learning of Preferential Attitude in Multi-Criteria Decision Making. *Proceedings of the 7th International Symposium on Methodologies for Intelligent Systems*: 642-651.

Slowinski, R., Stefanowski, J. 1996. Rough-set reasoning about uncertain data. *Fundamenta Informaticae*, 27(2-3): 229-243.

Stinchcombe, A. L. 1965. Social structures and organizations. In J. G. March (Ed.), *Handbook of Organizations*: 142-193. Chicago, IL.: Rand McNally.

Tversky, A., Kahneman, D. 1974. Judgment under Uncertainty: Heuristics and Biases. *Science*, 185: 1124- 1131.

Tyebjee, T. T., Bruno, A. V. 1984. A Model of Venture Capitalist Investment Activity. *Management Science*, 30(9): 1051-1066.

Weller, S. C., Romney, A. K. 1988. *Systematic Data Collection*. Beverly Hills, CA: Sage Publications. Williamson, O. E. 1985. *The Economic Institutions of Capitalism: Firms, Markets, Relational Contracting*. New York: Free Press.

Zacharakis, A. L., Meyer, G. D. 1998. A lack of insight: do venture capitalists really understand their own decision process? *Journal of Business Venturing*, 13(1): 57-76.

Zacharakis, A. L., Meyer, G. D. 2000. The potential of actuarial decision models: Can they improve the venture capital investment decision? *Journal of Business Venturing*, 15(4): 323-346.

Zacharakis, A. L., Shepherd, D. A. 2001. The nature of information and overconfidence on venture capitalists' decision making. *Journal of Business Venturing*, 16(4): 311-332.

Zsambok, C. E., Klein, G. 1996. Naturalistic decision making. NJ: Lawrence Erlbaum.

End Notes

[1] The medical environment presents "ill structured problems, uncertain dynamic environments, shifting, ill-defined or competing goals, time stress and high risk as well as issues associated with multiple players" (Patel et al. 1996).

[2] To our knowledge there were no industry shocks to bias expert evaluations in 2004 and 2005, and because much of the funding was for startups, it is highly unlikely that startups were successful within a year to bias the expert's knowledge about potential of a product or service.

[3] Two experts did not provide complete evaluation of the unfunded business plan, thus the final sample consisted of 72 funded and 71 non-funded business plans.

[4] We made certain that the experts did not have any more information about these businesses than was available in the business plans; they were not familiar with the businesses they evaluated.

[5] Assumption of the underlying distribution is critical to understand the latent structure because of the potential of underlying heterogeneity at the individual decision level and VC firm level. Ventures invested in are heterogeneous in nature in terms of industry potential and other external dimensions.

[6] Many latent class MDS techniques have been identified in marketing Sinha and DeSarbo (1988) However, these techniques are based on market segments of consumers that may not be easily discernible in the case of the VC industry. Moreover, VC syndicate networks may mean that segmentation among VC firms may not be as distinct as possible. The cross interaction of the nature of venture under consideration may increase heterogeneity but it may not be as discrete as a market segment in marketing. However, it is necessary to control for such heterogeneity.

[7] Based on popular recommendation Borgatti (1996, 1998) and Carroll and Chang (1969) and the nature of attribute scale we use metric PRO-FIT approach, wherein a set of multiple regressions are run using dependent variable (each attribute), and independent variables at each point in space.

[8] This approach is widely accepted and used in the finance literature predicting failure [9] http://ic.arc.nasa.gov/ic/projects/bayes-group/autoclass/

[10] The class divergence, or cross entropy with respect to the single class Classification, is a measure of how strongly the class probability distribution function differs from that of the database as a whole. It is zero for identical distributions, going infinite when two discrete distributions place probability 1 on differing values of the same attribute.

[11] I-jk denotes the term influence value for attribute k in class j. This is the cross entropy or KullbackLeibler distance between the class and full database probability distributions

In: Venture Capital and Angel Investing   ISBN: 978-1-61324-122-6
Editors: A. M. Lane, N. P. Mifflin   © 2011 Nova Science Publishers, Inc.

Chapter 2

THE IMPORTANCE OF ANGEL INVESTING IN FINANCING THE GROWTH OF ENTREPRENEURIAL VENTURES*

Scott Shane and Shaker Heights

ACKNOWLEDGMENT[1]

This report was developed under a contract with the Small Business Administration, Office of Advocacy, and contains information and analysis that was reviewed and edited by officials of the Office of Advocacy. However, the final conclusions of the report do not necessarily reflect the views of the Office of Advocacy.

---

* This is an edited, reformatted and augmented version of a working paper for Ofiice of
  Advocacy publication, dated September 2008.
[1] This Small Business Research Summary summarizes one of a series of working papers
  issued by the U.S. Small Business Administration's Office of Advocacy. The opinions and
  recommendations of the authors of this study do not necessarily reflect official policies of
  the SBA or other agencies of the U.S. government. For more information, write to the
  Office of Advocacy at 409 Third Street S.W., Washington, DC 20416, or visit the office's
  Internet site at www.sba.gov/advo.

INTRODUCTION

Many observers consider angel investments to be one of the key drivers behind the startup and the growth of new businesses, despite a paucity of information to confirm whether or not this is true. Unlike venture capital investments, angel investments are made by individual investors who do not make up a known population. Therefore, much of what is reported about angel investing comes from anecdotes and surveys of convenience samples, which are prone to biases and inaccuracies. Moreover, research on angel investment is plagued by definitional confusion, in which different investigators confound informal investors, friends and family who invest in startups, accredited and unaccredited angel investors, and individual and group investing. The variation makes it difficult to compare findings across studies.

PURPOSE

This report seeks to provide an accurate understanding of the role of angel investing in the entrepreneurial finance system. It provides a definition of angel investing and reviews the current state of understanding of the phenomenon, focusing on answering four questions: (1) How large is the angel capital market? (2) How much demand is there for angel capital? (3) What are the primary characteristics of angel investments? (4) What do the companies that receive angel financing look like? Among other databases, the study draws on the Survey of Business Owners (SBO); the Business Information Tracking Series (BITS); the Entrepreneurship in the United States Assessment (EUSA); the survey of the members of the Angel Capital Association (ACA); the Federal Reserve Survey of Small Business Finances (FRSSBF); and the Global Entrepreneurship Monitor (GEM).

OVERALL FINDINGS

The angel capital market is smaller than is generally believed. Few companies are appropriate for angel financing, a fact that limits demand for this source of financing. Angel investments are smaller and less sophisticated and include more debt than is commonly thought. And the companies that receive angel financing are more similar to typical startups.

HIGHLIGHTS

- According to the EUSA and GEM data, the estimated number of people who made an angel investment between 2001 and 2003 is between 331,100 and 629,000 people.

- According to estimates based on the EUSA data, between 2001 and 2003, angels invested an estimated $23 billion per year.

- Estimates based on several sources suggest that most angel investors are unaccredited investors, but that accredited investors provide the majority of dollars invested.

- Estimates based on data from the EUSA and the 2003 FRSSBF suggest that the number of companies that receive angel investments annually is between 50,700 and 57,300.

- According to the ACA, in 2006, the 5,632 accredited angel investors that make up its member groups made 947 investments in 512 companies, providing startups with a total of $228.8 million.

- According to estimates from the BITS, 3,608 companies founded in 1996 achieved the $10 million or more in sales by 2002 that many experts say angels' target.

- According to the EUSA data, the typical angel investment made between 2001 and 2003 was $10,000.

- According to the ACA, in 2006, the average dollar value invested per angel in an angel group deal was $31,457.

- According to the EUSA data, debt accounts for 40.2 percent of the money angels provided to startups between 2001 and 2003.

- Estimates based on the 2003 FRSSBF and the EUSA data suggest that between 0.17 and 0.2 percent of the companies financed by angels go public, and between 0.8 and 1.3 percent are acquired.

- Estimates of the rate of return net of opportunity cost of high-net-worth accredited angels affiliated with groups and willing to talk about their investments is 19.2 percent, according to data from the Angel Investor Performance Project (AIPP).

- According to the EUSA data, 25 percent of angel investments made between 2001 and 2003 went into retail businesses, and 12.5 percent went into personal service businesses.

- According to the 2003 FRSSBF, the typical business of any age—the average age was 13.3 years— that received an informal equity investment in the previous year had sales of $435,000, employment of seven, and profits of $7,500.

- According to data from the 2002 SBO, only 11 percent of firms that were five years old or younger and had received an external equity investment had a female primary owner, only 3.8 percent had an Hispanic primary owner, and only 1.4 percent had a Black primary owner.

- According to data from the 2002 SBO, over two-thirds of the entrepreneurs whose businesses had received an external equity investment and were less than six years old were between the ages of 35 and 54 years.

SCOPE AND METHODOLOGY

This study reviewed the literature, including published books and articles, as well as unpublished reports. It also involved a statistical evaluation of data sources drawn from representative samples of known populations the SBO (through special tabulations); the BITS (through special tabulations); the EUSA; the survey of the ACA members; the Federal Reserve Survey of Consumer Finances (FRSCF); the FRSSBF; the GEM; and the Kauffman Firm Study (KFS)—not previously used to examine angel investing in the United States. The study also examined new, nonrepresentative surveys of angel investors, such as the AIPP. Finally, it compared the results of these analyses to previous studies of nonrepresentative samples of business angels.

OVERVIEW

Investigation of the role of angel investing in financing private businesses in the United States is important.[1] Many observers consider angel investments to be one of the key drivers behind the startup and the growth of new businesses,[2] despite a paucity of information to confirm whether or not this is true. Unlike venture capital investments, angel investments are made by individual investors who do not make up a known population. Therefore, much of what is reported about angel investing comes from anecdotes and surveys of convenience samples, which are prone to biases and inaccuracies. Moreover, research on this topic is plagued by definitional confusion, in which different investigators confound informal investors, friends and family who invest in start-ups, accredited and unaccredited angel investors, and individual and group investing; this confusion makes it difficult to compare findings across studies.

This report seeks to provide an accurate understanding of the role of angel investing in the entrepreneurial finance system. It provides a definition of angel investing, and reviews the current state of understanding of the phenomenon, focusing on answering four questions: (1) How large is the angel capital market? (2) How much demand is there for angel capital? (3) What are the primary characteristics of angel investments? (4) What do the companies that receive angel financing look like?

To answer this question, the author reviewed the literature, including published books and articles, as well as unpublished reports. The study also includes a statistical evaluation of data sources drawn from representative samples of known populations—the Survey of Business Owners (SBO) (through special tabulations); the Business Information Tracking Series (BITS) (through special tabulations); the Entrepreneurship in the United States Assessment (EUSA); the survey of the members of the Angel Capital Association (ACA); the Federal Reserve Survey of Consumer Finances (FRSCF); the Federal Reserve Survey of Small Business Finances (FRSSBF); the Global

Entrepreneurship Monitor (GEM); and the Kauffman Firm Study (KFS)—not previously used to examine angel investing in the United States. I also examined new, nonrepresentative surveys of angel investors, such as the Angel Investment Performance Project (AIPP). Finally, I compared the results of these analyses to previous studies of nonrepresentative samples of business angels.

The primary findings are:

- According to the EUSA and GEM data, the estimated number of people who made an angel investment between 2001 and 2003 is between 331,100 and 629,000 people.
- According to estimates based on the EUSA data, between 2001 and 2003, angels invested an estimated $23 billion per year.
- Estimates based on several sources suggest that the majority of angel investors are unaccredited investors, but that accredited investors provide the majority of dollars invested.

- Estimates based on data from the EUSA and the 2003 FRSSBF suggest that the number of companies that receive angel investments annually is between 50,700 and 57,300.
- According to the ACA, in 2006, the 5,632 accredited angel investors that make up its member groups made 947 investments in 512 companies, providing start-ups with a total of $228.8 million.[3]
- According to estimates from the BITS, 3,608 companies founded in 1996 achieved the $10 million or more in sales by 2002 that many experts say angels target.
- According to the EUSA data, the typical angel investment made between 2001 and 2003 was $10,000.
- According to the ACA, in 2006, the average dollar value invested per angel in an angel group deal was $31,457.
- According to the EUSA data, debt accounted for 40.2 percent of the money angels provided to startups between 2001 and 2003. Estimates based on the 2003 FRSSBF and the EUSA data suggest that between 0.17 and 0.2 percent of the companies financed by angels go public, and between 0.8 and 1.3 percent are acquired.
- Estimates of the rate of return net of opportunity cost of high-net-worth accredited angels affiliated with groups and willing to talk about their investments is 19.2 percent, according to data from the AIPP.
- According to the EUSA data, 25 percent of angel investments made between 2001 and 2003 went into retail businesses, and 12.5 percent went into personal service businesses.
- According to the 2003 FRSSBF, the typical business of any age—the average age was 13.3 years—that received an informal equity investment in the previous year had sales of $435,000, employment of seven, and profits of $7,500.
- According to data from the 2002 SBO, only 11 percent of firms that were five years old or younger and had received an external equity investment had a female primary owner; only 3.8 percent had an Hispanic primary owner, and only 1.4 percent had a Black primary owner.
- According to data from the 2002 SBO, over two-thirds of the entrepreneurs whose businesses had received an external equity investment and were less than six years old were between the ages of 35 and 54 years.

The study makes two contributions to public policy. First, it provides more accurate estimates of the market for angel capital, the demand for angel capital, the companies that receive angel capital, and angel deals than were previously available. These data provide the facts that policymakers need to develop ways to enhance the growth of entrepreneurship in the United States.

Second, the report provides insight into the role of public policy in the angel capital market. The information from this study will allow policymakers to evaluate the importance of the angel capital market to entrepreneurial activity in the United States, and the need for policy intervention. In addition, it provides insight into the investment activity of different groups of angel investors (e.g., accredited and unaccredited investors), which will be useful in predicting how angel investors might respond to public policy toward angel investing.

However, the data on which all discussions of angel investing are based are flawed, leading researchers to draw inferences from either nonrepresentative convenience samples or small representative samples, both of which can lead to inaccurate estimates (although for different reasons.) A truly accurate understanding of angel investing will require the creation of large representative samples of angel investors, angel investments, and angel-financed companies.

INTRODUCTION

Investigation of the role of angel investing in financing private businesses in the United States is important. Many observers consider angel investments to be one of the key drivers behind the startup and growth of new businesses,[4] despite a paucity of information to confirm whether or not this is true. Unlike venture capital investments, angel investments are made by individual investors who do not make up a known population. Therefore, much of what is reported about angel investing comes from anecdotes and surveys of convenience samples, which are prone to biases and inaccuracies. Moreover, research on this topic is plagued by definitional confusion, in which different investigators confound informal investors, friends and family who invest in startups, accredited and unaccredited angel investors, and individual and group investing; this confusion makes it difficult to compare findings across studies.

This report seeks to provide an accurate understanding of the role of angel investing in the entrepreneurial finance system. It defines angel investing and reviews the current state of understanding of the phenomenon, focusing on answering four questions: (1) How large is the angel capital market? (2) How much demand is there for angel capital? (3) What are the primary characteristics of angel investments? (4) What do the companies that receive angel financing look like? It answers these questions by reviewing the literature, providing a statistical evaluation of data sources drawn from representative samples of known populations, examining new nonrepresentative surveys of angel investors, and comparing the results of these new analyses to previous studies of nonrepresentative samples of business angels.

DEFINITIONS

Because of the definitional confusion that plagues research on angel investing, this report begins with some definitions. An angel investor is *a person who provides capital, in the form of debt or equity, from his own funds to a private business owned and operated by someone else who is neither a friend nor a family member.*

Business angels are far from the only source of external capital entrepreneurs can tap. The entrepreneur's friends and family, institutional investors such as venture capitalists and banks, trade creditors, and a host of other entities provide capital to private businesses. Therefore, it is important to differentiate angel investors from other sources of capital. To minimize the confusion about who is an angel investor and who is not, the following definitions are provided:

- Institutional investor: A corporation, financial institution, or other organization (e.g., venture capital firm) that uses money raised from another party to provide capital to a private business owned and operated by someone else.
- Friends and family investor: An individual who uses his own money to provide capital to a private business owned and operated by a family member, work colleague, friend, or neighbor.
- Informal investor: An individual (not an institution) who uses his own money to provide capital to a private business owned and operated by someone else.

The most important point about angel investing that comes from these definitions is the following: every angel is an informal investor, but not every informal investor is an angel. That is, informal investors are made up of two different groups of investors, angels *and* friends and family.

Another important point that comes from these definitions is the heterogeneity among angel investors. Some angels are accredited investors,[5] while others are not. Some angels are early-stage capital providers, while others put money into businesses that are cash flow positive at the time of investment. Some angels are passive investors, conducting little, if any, due diligence of potential investments, and having scant involvement with the companies or founders after they invest, while others undertake more detailed due diligence and get actively involved with the companies that they finance. Some angels are quite knowledgeable about investing in private companies, while others are quite naïve about entrepreneurship. Some angels take high risks to earn high returns, while others seek lower risks and lower returns. Some angels invest alone, while others invest as part of an organized group. These different dimensions affect the range of businesses in which angels invest, the organizational arrangements that they employ, their investment criteria, their decision-making processes, and a host of other things that make describing business angels quite difficult.

Debt Versus Equity Investments

Angel investments include debt as well as equity. Because angels, unlike venture capitalists, have no fiduciary responsibility to other investors and are not regulated, as is the case for banks, angels can and do invest using a very wide range of financial instruments, from pure debt to pure equity. For instance, some highly sophisticated accredited angel investors affiliated with organized angel groups report using debt instruments, particularly convertible debt, when investing in seed stage companies.[6]

The use of debt instruments is not restricted to the use of convertible debt. In focus groups on angel investing sponsored by five Federal Reserve regional banks, several highly sophisticated angels reported that they had made investments as large as $150,000 in unsecured debt.[7] Moreover, earlier quantitative studies point to the use of debt by informal investors. For instance, Robert Gaston's 1989 study of informal equity investments in the United States showed that 41.2 percent of the money received by companies that had received an informal equity investment took the form of debt.[8]

Active Versus Passive Investors

Previous research shows that many angels are passive investors. For instance, one study of a sample of accredited angel investors who appear in the database of a consulting firm showed that 35 percent would make an early-stage angel investment *without* looking at the entrepreneur's business plan.[9] Other studies report that 20 percent of angels performed *no* due diligence on investments that they made. 10

Data from the Angel Investor Performance Project (AIPP) indicate that many angels do not get actively involved with their ventures after investing. A study by Robert Wiltbank using these data showed that the bottom third of the sample spent only two hours per week on their ventures.[11] This number translates to less than eight minutes per week of post-investment involvement per venture.

Experienced Versus Inexperienced Investors

One-time investors are included in the population of investors for this study. There are several reasons for not restricting angel investors to those who make more than one investment. First, studies of wealthy individuals known to make equity investments in early-stage technology companies—the "traditional" definition of an "angel" investor— show that a significant minority have made only one investment in their lifetimes. For instance, one study showed that 35 percent of these types of business angels had made only a single investment.[12] Similarly, the data from the AIPP show that 10 percent of high net worth (averaging $10.9 million) angel investors who participate in organized angel groups have made only a single angel investment.

Second, the more representative Entrepreneurship in the United States (EUSA) data indicate that 20.8 percent of the people who had made an angel investment in the previous three years had made only one informal investment in their careers.

Third, anecdotal evidence suggests that one-time angels can be successful investors in startup companies. For example, the angel investment that is believed to have the highest return on capital invested—that made by Iain McGlinn in the Body Shop[13]— was made by an investor with no prior investments in startup companies.

Fourth, by definition, all angel investors, including the very most successful ones such as Andrew Flipowski, who made $24 million from an investment in Blue Rhino; Andy Bechtolscheim, who made hundreds of millions of dollars from his investment in Google; and Thomas Alberg, the angel investor who earned $26 million from his investment in Amazon.com,[14] all had once made a single angel investment.

High Technology Versus Low Technology Businesses

Angel investing includes investments made in companies in all industries. Many experts explain that angels invest in companies in low-technology industries. For example, Ian Sobieski, the managing member of the Band of Angels explains,

> Angels, by some numbers, invest a total amount of money larger than the formal venture capital industry....Most of that money does not go into high-tech start-ups that get fed into the venture capital channel. Most of that money goes into other things. The amount of money going into high-tech equity is only a small part of that....They might invest in the local McDonald's franchise, or the roller rink, or the trendy restaurant downtown or the restoration of the artsy theater. Those are all angels—individuals that invest their own money.[15]

Moreover, several low-technology companies founded in industries in which most startups are not high growth have generated extremely high financial returns on angel investments, such as Starbucks and Kinko's. Because angels can and do make successful investments in low-technology companies in slow-growth industries, it does not make sense to exclude these investments from the angel investment population.

Definitions of Subsets of Business Angels

To mitigate confusion about angel investors, several key categories of angel investors are defined.

Unaccredited and Accredited Investors

- Unaccredited angel investor: An individual who does not meet the Securities and Exchange Commission's (SEC) accreditation requirements and who uses his or her own money to provide capital to a private business owned and operated by someone else, who is neither a friend nor a family member.
- Accredited angel investor: An individual who meets SEC accreditation requirements and who uses his or her own money to provide capital to a private business owned and operated by someone else, who is neither a friend nor a family member.

Active and Passive Investors

- Active angel investor: An individual who uses his or her own money to provide capital to a private business owned and operated by someone else, who is neither a friend nor family member, and who invests time as well as money in the development of the company.
- Passive angel investor: An individual uses his / her own money to provide capital to a private business owned and operated by someone else, who is neither a friend nor a family member, but who does not invest time in the development of the company.[16]

Individual Angels and Angel Groups

- Individual angel: A person who acts on his / her own to provide some of his money to a private business owned and operated by someone else, who is neither a friend nor a family member.
- Angel group member: A person who acts as part of a group to provide some of his / her own money to a private business owned and operated by someone else, who is neither a friend nor a family member.

PROBLEMS WITH PREVIOUS RESEARCH ON ANGEL INVESTING

Previous research has not adequately addressed the questions policymakers have about angel investing for several reasons. First, there is remarkably little primary research on angel investing in the United States. Although there are a handful of practitioner articles in which angels reflect upon their experience as angel investors, a few descriptions of angel groups and angel investment programs, some business school teaching notes, and an occasional newspaper or magazine article that interviews a business angel, there is almost no qualitative or quantitative data on angel investing.

Second, a significant portion of primary research on angel investing takes the form of qualitative research. While these studies provide useful information, they suffer from two important limitations: All are based on convenience samples that cannot be generalized to the overall population of angel investors in the United States; and none involve a control group or a large enough number of angel investors to make hypothesis testing possible.

Third, the large-sample databases that have been used to examine angel investing in the past—for instance, the annual survey conducted by the Center for Venture Research at the University of New Hampshire—rely on convenience samples drawn disproportionately from angel groups. They do not accurately represent angels who make individual investments, because unaccredited angel investors are excluded from angel groups to comply with Securities and Exchange Commission (SEC) regulations. In addition, they are not available to other investigators, making it impossible to verify the accuracy of the findings claimed by the researchers or to evaluate the reliability, validity, and representativeness of the data.

Fourth, prior studies do not examine several important aspects of angel investing. For instance, no studies have examined the unaccredited angel market although several data sources indicate that unaccredited investors make up a sizeable portion of angel investors.

RESEARCH DESIGN

This study overcomes the limitations of prior studies of angel investing by examining new, more reliable, valid, and representative datasets than those used previously. The primary data sources used in this study are:

1. The U.S portion of the Global Entrepreneurship Monitor (GEM), a series of annual surveys conducted with a representative sample of the adult-aged population in a variety of countries from 1998 through 2003.

2. The Entrepreneurship in the United States Assessment (EUSA), a representative survey of U.S. adults conducted in 2004.

3. The Kauffman Firm Study (KFS), a representative survey of new, for-profit, independent businesses started in the United States in 2004 that were drawn from a Dun and Bradstreet sampling frame and adjusted to include only businesses that did not receive an employer identification number; report schedule C income; establish a legal form; or pay state unemployment or federal social security taxes prior to 2004.

4. The 2004 Federal Reserve Survey of Consumer Finances (FRSCF), a survey of financial characteristics of a representative sample of approximately 4,500 U.S. households that is conducted every three years by the Federal Reserve. (The report also draws on previously published research that examines earlier years of the FRSCF).

5. The (2002) Federal Reserve Survey of Small Business Finances (FRSSBF), a survey of a representative sample of small businesses in the United States, drawn from a Dun and Bradstreet sampling frame. This study will examine primarily the 2003 survey. (The report also draws on previously published research that examines earlier years of the FRSSBF).

6. A special tabulation of businesses founded between 1997 and 2001 from the Survey of Business Owners (SBO), a survey of all employer and nonemployer businesses operating in the United States in 2002.

7. The Wisconsin Department of Revenue records on the use of the state's angel tax credit (WATC) in 2005.

8. The Federal Reserve Angel Focus Group Study (FRAFG), a study consisting of four two-and-a-half hour focus group sessions conducted in 2005 with eight to ten business angels each in Atlanta, Cleveland, Denver, and Philadelphia identified by representatives of the Federal Reserve regional banks through a snowball sampling procedure in which existing study subjects are used to recruit more subjects into the sample.

9. The Angel Capital Association (ACA) Surveys of its member groups from 2004 through 2007.

10. The Business Information Tracking Series (BITS) of the U.S. Bureau of the Census on the sales of the 1996 cohort of new single-unit establishments from 1997 through 2002.
11. The Angel Investment Performance Project (AIPP), a survey of angel investors associated with groups on the performance of the angel investments from which they have exited.

The study also makes use of statistics published by researchers using other datasets. For instance, it includes information published by Dr. Andrew Wong about 143 businesses that received an investment from a business angel between 1994 and 2001. Finally, the study uses published statistics (with caveats, given the limitations of these data) produced from the annual survey conducted by the Center for Venture Research (CVR).

ANALYTIC TECHNIQUES USED

The data from primary sources were examined in two ways. First, descriptive statistics were produced from the datasets. Second, regression analysis was conducted on some of the datasets. However, the small sample sizes limit the power of the regression analysis. Therefore, the reported results take the form of descriptive statistics.

As Table 1 shows, the datasets on which inferences about angel investments are drawn for this report include relatively small numbers of business angels, angel investments, and angel-backed companies, making the estimates reported here imprecise. (The sources include much larger numbers of informal investments, informal investors, and informal investor-backed companies. So this imprecision is not present for those estimates.) To minimize inaccurate estimates, I seek convergence across results from multiple datasets. In addition, I compare the estimates for angel investment activity to estimates for the larger populations of which angels are a part to test the consistency between estimates from small samples with estimates from larger samples. Both of these approaches increase confidence in the results.

THE ANGEL CAPITAL MARKET

As defined earlier, an angel investor is a person who provides capital, in the form of debt or equity, from his own funds to a private business owned and operated by someone else who is neither a friend nor a family member. Measuring angel investing is difficult. As Table 1 shows, only two data sources include information from a representative sample and measure angel investing—EUSA and GEM. (The FRSSBF includes information from a representative sample on a subset of angel investing, those angels who make equity investments in companies.)

Three dimensions of the angel capital market are the amount of capital provided, the number of investors, and the number of companies receiving financing.

The Number of Angel Investors

Angel investing is a small part of the informal capital market. The operational definition of an angel investor in the GEM and EUSA data is a person who made an informal investment in the previous three years in a business run by someone other than a friend or family member. Analysis of data from the EUSA indicates that only 8 percent of the investments were made in a business run by "a stranger with a good idea," rather than in a business run by a friend or family member. The GEM data corroborate this estimate. Approximately 8.5 percent of the investments made by U.S. respondents to the GEM survey about their informal investments made from 1998 to 2003 were made in businesses not run by a friend or family member. Similarly, the 2003 SSBF reveals that 7.4 percent of the *equity* investments by nonfounders received by companies in the previous 12 months came from "angel investors."

The EUSA data gathered in 2004 show that of the overall population of adults, 0.2 percent made an angel investment in the previous three years. The GEM data, measured over the 1998-2003 period, show that 0.3 percent of U.S. adults made an angel investment in the previous three years. Approximately 0.1 percent of adults who were surveyed in the EUSA made an angel equity investment in the previous three years; however, the sample size for this estimate is very small.

Table 1. The Sample Sizes of the Data Sources Used in this Report[1]

Survey[2]	Date	Sample Size	Informal Investor[3]	Informal Equity[4]	External Investor[5]	External Equity Investor[6]	Angel Investor[7]	Angel Equity Investor[8]
EUSA (Investor)	2004	13,891	492	112	117	64	26	19
EUSA (Deal)[9]	2004	315	315	129	160	87	33	23
FRSSBF	2003	4,240		114				8
SBO	2002	322,327				4,123		
FRSCF	2004	4,522		67				
KFS	2004	4,930		185		85		
GEM	1998-2003	23,077	1,079		385		71	

[1] An empty cell means that no information is available. Because of missing cases, the percentages of the sample in each subsample do not correspond to the reported estimates.

[2] The data from the EUSA, SBO, and GEM are unweighted; the data from the FRSSBF, FRSCF, and KFS are weighted. When the data are weighted, the weights are recentered for the subsample examined. The FRSSBF includes five "implicates" that include different values for imputed variables. Because it is unclear which imputation procedure is appropriate for these analyses, all "implicates" are used in the calculations.

[3] Informal investor is an individual (not an institution) who used his own money to provide capital to a private business owned and operated by someone else. For the EUSA data, this investment was measured as the incidence of investment by a U.S. adult from 2001-2003 in a business owned by an immediate family member, other relative, friend, coworker, neighbor, or stranger. For the GEM data, this investment was measured as the incidence of investment by a U.S. adult made over the three previous years with data collected annually from 1998 to 2003 in a business owned by an immediate family member, other relative, friend, coworker, neighbor, or stranger.

[4] Informal equity investor is an individual (not an institution) who used his own money to make an equity investment in a private business owned and operated by someone else. For the EUSA data, this investment was measured as the incidence of investment by a U.S. adult from 2001 to 2003 in a business owned by an immediate family member, other relative, friend, coworker, neighbor, or stranger. For the GEM data, this investment was measured as the incidence of investment

by a U.S. adult made over the three previous years with data collected annually from 1998 to 2003 in a business owned by an immediate family member, other relative, friend, co-worker, neighbor, or stranger. For the FRSSBF, informal equity was measured as the receipt of an equity investment from individual investors by a company with fewer than 500 employees in the previous 12 months. For the FRSCF, informal equity was measured as ownership by a U.S. household of a business that is not actively managed by someone in the household. For the KFS, informal equity was measured as the receipt of an equity investment in its first year of operation by a noninstitutional investor who was not a member of the founding team in a for-profit business founded in 2004 that was not a branch or subsidiary owned by an existing business, was newly listed in Dun and Bradstreet's directories, and did not have an employer identification number, schedule C income, a legal form, or paid state unemployment insurance or federal social security taxes prior to 2004.

[5] An external investor is an individual (not an institution) who used his own money to provide capital to a private business owned and operated by a relative. For the EUSA data, this investment was measured as the incidence of investment by a U.S. adult from 2001 to 2003 in a business run by a friend, neighbor, coworker or stranger. For the GEM data, this investment was measured as the incidence of investment by a U.S. adult made over the three previous years with data collected annually from 1998 to 2003 in a business run by a friend, neighbor, coworker or stranger.

[6] An external equity investor is an individual (not an institution) who used his own money to make an investment in a private business owned and operated by a relative. For the EUSA data, this investment was measured as the incidence of equity investment by a U.S. adult from 2001 to 2003 in a business owned by an immediate family member, other relative, friend, coworker, neighbor, or stranger. For the GEM data, this investment was measured as the incidence of investment by a U.S. adult made over the three previous years with data collected annually from 1998 to 2003 in a business owned by an immediate family member, other relative, friend, coworker, neighbor, or stranger. For the SBO, informal equity was measured as employer businesses that were established, purchased, or acquired in 1997, 1998, 1999, 2000, or 2001 for which owner 1 owned less than 100 percent and owners 2 or 3 spent no hours managing or working in the business; the business was not exclusively owned by members of the same family; and funds were received from an outside investor. For the KFS, external equity was measured as the receipt of an equity investment in its first year of operation by a noninstitutional investor who was not a member of the founding team in a for-profit business founded in 2004 that was not a branch or subsidiary owned by an existing business, was newly listed in Dun and Bradstreet's directories, and did not have an employer identification number, schedule C income, a legal form or had paid state unemployment insurance or federal social security taxes prior to 2004.

[7] Angel investor is an individual (not an institution) who used his own money to provide capital to a private business owned and operated by someone else who is neither a friend nor a family member. For the EUSA data, this investment was measured as the incidence of investment by a U.S. adult from 2001 to 2003 in a business owned by a stranger. For the GEM data, this investment was measured as the incidence of investment by a U.S. adult made over the three previous years with data collected annually from 1998 to 2003 in a business owned by a stranger.

[8] Angel equity investor is an individual (not an institution) who used his own money to make an equity investment in a private business owned and operated by someone else who is neither a friend nor a family member. For the EUSA data, this investment was measured as the incidence of equity investment by a U.S. adult from 2001 to 2003 in a business owned by a stranger. For the GEM data, this investment was measured as the incidence of equity investment by a U.S. adult made over the three previous years with data collected annually from 1998 to 2003 in a business owned by a stranger. For the FRSSBF, informal equity was measured as the receipt of an equity investment from individual investors by a company with fewer than 500 employees in the previous 12 months in which the respondents categorized the individual investors as "angel investors."

[9] The respondents to the EUSA were asked if they made an informal investment in the previous three years. If they answered "yes", they were asked to describe up to three investments that they made over that period. The respondents were asked to identify whether each investment was made in a business owned by a friend, neighbor or coworker, immediate family member, other family member, or stranger. This information was used to determine whether the individual had made an angel investment during the previous three years. Because respondents could have reported on up to three angel investments, the EUSA contains information on more angel "deals" than angel investors.

These numbers are much smaller than the portion of the U.S. adult age population who made an informal investment between 2001 and 2003. The EUSA showed that 3.5 percent of the adult-aged population made an informal investment over this period. Because there were 212 million adult Americans in 2003, the estimates from the GEM and EUSA mean that an estimated 7.4 million U.S. adults made an informal investment between 2001 and 2003.[17]

Multiplying the estimated 7.4 million U.S. adults who made an informal investment between 2001 and 2003 by the proportion of informal investments that are angel investments found in the EUSA and GEM datasets yields an estimate of between 592,000 and 629,000 people who made an angel investment in the 2001-2003 period. However, an estimate of the number of people who made an angel investment from 2001- 2003 based on the EUSA counts of angel investors yields an estimated 331,100 people. In short, these different ways of estimating the number of business angels reveal an estimated range in the number of angel investors from 331,100 to 629,000.[18]

The number of investors estimated from the EUSA and GEM data are considerably higher than the number of investors estimated by the Center for Venture Research at the University of New Hampshire (CVR), which reported 220,000 "active" angel investors in 2003.[19] However, the CVR defines "active" angel investors as people who made an angel investment in the previous 12 months. Adjusting the EUSA and GEM data to conform to the CVR definition, gives comparable estimates for the number of active angel investors.[20] The EUSA and GEM data generate estimates of 140,000 to 266,000 "active" angel investors in one of the three years covered by the study. That is, measured on an "active" angel basis, the numbers from the EUSA and GEM databases are in a similar range to those provided by the CVR.[21]

The Number of Companies Receiving Angel Investment

It is possible to extrapolate to the number of companies receiving angel investments in the United States every year from data on angel investments made by respondents to the EUSA. This extrapolation yields an estimate of angel investments in approximately 57,300 companies per year. Limiting the estimate to those companies that received an equity investment from a business angel produces an extrapolation of 49,800.[22]

This estimate is close to the estimate of the number of companies receiving angel investments every year extrapolated from the 2003 FRSSBF, which found that 0.19 percent of U.S. businesses with fewer than 500 employees had "received an equity investment from a business angel in the previous 12 months."[23] The FRSSBF number extrapolates to 44,100 companies that received an angel equity investment in the previous 12 months. Adjusting the FRSSBF estimate by the proportion of angel investments that do not involve equity produces an estimate of 50,700 companies that receive an investment from a business angel each year.

The estimates from the FRSSBF and the EUSA are similar to those reported for 2003 and 2004 by the CVR, which found that 39,000 companies received an angel investment in 2003 and 48,000 companies received such an investment in 2004,[24] or an average of 43,500 across the two years. Assuming that the CVR measures only companies that receive *equity* investments from business angels, its numbers are consistent with the 49,800 companies that receive angel equity investments estimated from the EUSA and the 44,100 companies estimated from the FRSSBF.[25]

The Amount of Angel Capital Invested

Estimates of the size of the angel capital market calculated from the proportion of informal investments that are angel investments,[26] weighted by the different median sizes of angel and friends and family investments as indicated by the EUSA data, yield an estimated value of $23 billion in angel investment per year.[27] Calculating the dollar amount of angel investment from the average investment multiplied by the average number of investors per company and the number of companies estimated to receive an angel investment annually yields $21.4 billion.[28]

Estimating the dollar value of the angel capital market in the United States from the GEM data yields a lower estimated value of $12.7 billion per year.[29]

It is also possible to estimate the dollar value of the angel capital market in the United States by examining the data from the FRSSBF on the ratio of venture capital to angel capital received by small businesses. A study that looked at these data found that 3.6 percent of the capital that the companies had received had come from business angels, compared with 1.9 percent from venture capitalists.[30] Multiplying the ratio of angel equity investment to venture capital equity investment by estimates of the amount of venture capital investment made in 2003 produces an estimated $36 billion per year in capital invested by business angels.[31]

These estimates are comparable to those found by the CVR. The dollar value of annual flows of angel capital calculated in different ways from the EUSA, GEM and FRSSBF ($12.7 billion to $36 billion) bound the estimate provided by the CVR, which reported $18.1 billion in business angel investment in 2003.[32]

TWO SUBSETS OF ANGEL INVESTORS

Two important subsets of angel investors are angel groups and accredited angel investors.

Angel Groups

Recently, accredited angel investors have begun to invest collectively in "angel groups." Observers estimate the number of these groups in the United States to be between 125 and 300.[33] About half of all known angel groups have banded together to form a trade association called the Angel Capital Association (ACA).[34]

Angel group members are a minority of all business angels operating in the United States. In 2006, the angel groups that participatee in the Angel Capital Association were composed of 5,632 angel investors.[35] In 2006, the groups that were the members of the Angel Capital Association made 947 investments in 512 companies, providing start-ups with a total of $228.8 million.[36]

Users might have less confidence in the ACA data than some of the other sources of angel data provided in this report. The ACA is a trade association that angel groups can choose to join or not join. Therefore, the sample of groups in the ACA is probably not representative of the overall population of angel groups. Moreover, the ACA survey of its members is voluntary and subject to significant nonresponse. As a result, the means and other estimates reported by the ACA are based on the respondents and therefore might be biased because of the nonresponse of some groups.

Nevertheless, the ACA surveys of its members provide some basic demographics of angel groups. Each year, the average angel group invests in 3.8 companies. The average angel group investment is $241,528 per round.[37] The median age of a group is 3 years, and the average age is 4.2.[38] The average size is 47.6 members (median of 37).[39]

However, estimates from the ACA data indicate that only 17.5 percent of angel group members invest in each deal the group invests in.[40]

Unaccredited and Accredited Angel Investors

Only some angel investors meet the SEC income or net worth requirements necessary to be accredited investors.[41] At the level of the investors, only 23 percent of the people who made an investment in the previous three years in a business run by someone who is neither a friend nor a family member would meet SEC accreditation requirements. At the deal level, only 21 percent of the investments made in a private business run by someone who is neither a friend nor a family member from 2001 through 2003 were made by an investor who meets SEC accreditation requirements by either net worth or income.[42]

These numbers are hard to corroborate given the paucity of the data. However, the available data support the observation that most angel investors are not accredited investors. For instance, data from the GEM show that 8.3 percent of business angels were in the lowest third of income for Americans, and 21.7 percent were in the next third, leaving only 70 percent of angel investors in the top third of income in the United States (the cut off to enter the top third of U.S. income earners is only $75,000 per year, well below the level that makes someone an accredited investor).

Data from the state of Wisconsin's Revenue Division on taxpayers who took advantage of that state's angel tax credit in 2005 show that 52 percent of the tax filers who received an angel tax credit, and 54 percent of the tax filers who received a seed angel investment credit, had an adjusted gross income of less than $200,000 per year, the minimum for a single person to be an accredited investor.[43]

Accredited angel investors account for a larger portion of the *dollar value* of the angel capital market because their investments tend to be larger than those of unaccredited angels. Data from the EUSA suggest that accredited angels provide about 54 percent of the angel dollars invested annually. Data from the state of Wisconsin's Revenue Division on the taxpayers who took advantage of the state's angel tax credit in 2005 suggest a much higher accredited angel share of angel investment dollars. Investors with more than $200,000 in income accounted for 80.6 percent of the amount invested in businesses eligible for the angel tax credit in Wisconsin in 2005. However, these data need to be treated with caution because they are data from a single state, based on a tax credit that is limited to certain types of investments, and are estimated solely on the basis of income that reaches the accredited investor level only for a single person.[44]

DEMAND FOR ANGEL CAPITAL

Another approach to examining angel investing is to look at the demand for angel capital. An estimate of the demand for angel capital is based on the number of companies that need amounts of money that angels provide *and* that take a legal form in which an external equity investment is possible; the number of companies that look for angel capital every year; and the number of businesses with angel-appropriate growth rates.

The Number of Companies Needing the Appropriate Amount of Capital

Some experts say that companies seeking angel financing typically need between $25,000 and $500,000.[45] Approximately 15.1 percent of new business founders surveyed in the Entrepreneurship in the United States Assessment say that they need between $25,000 and $500,000 from an external source.

However, angels tend to invest only in corporations, rather than sole proprietorships or partnerships, because they want to make investments in entities from which they can exit with reasonable ease, and they generally want some mechanism to protect themselves against malfeasance and opportunistic behavior by entrepreneurs. In fact, data from the FRSSBF indicates that *only* businesses taking a corporate legal form had received an informal equity investment in the previous 12 months.

Therefore, the number of companies that demand angel investment can be estimated to be the count of businesses that need the amount of money that angels provide *and* have the appropriate legal form to receive an external equity investment. The number of new businesses founded every year that take a corporate form,[46] and need between $25,000 and $500,000 from someone other than the founder is estimated at 71,382 annually.

However, some observers believe that companies do not seek angel financing until their capital needs are significantly greater than $25,000. For example, business angels John May and Cal Simmons argue that entrepreneurs do not tend to look for money from business angels until their funding needs exceed $100,000.[47] At the same time, they say that companies generally need to go to venture capitalists when they need $2 million or more. If angels fund companies that need between $100,000 and $2 million, then only an estimated 31,279 new companies founded each year need the amount of money that angels can provide *and* take the appropriate legal form for angel financing.

The Number of Companies that Look for Angel Money

Another estimate of the demand for angel capital is based on the number of companies that seek angel money at any point in time. One study that examined data from the FRSSBF showed that only 4 percent of corporations *sought* an equity investment from a nonfounder during the previous three years.[48] Four percent of the number of corporations with fewer than 500 employees is 215,000 companies. The FRSSBF data also indicate that 7.4

percent of informal equity investments are angel equity investments. If the angel portion of companies that seek an informal equity investment is the same as the angel portion of companies that get an informal equity investment, then fewer than 16,000 small corporations sought an angel investment in the previous three years.

The Number of Firms with Angel-Appropriate Growth Rates

A third way to look at companies that are appropriate for angel capital is to look at the number of companies that display growth rates that fit the preferences of business angels. Experts typically describe angel-appropriate growth rates in terms of the level of sales achieved five to seven years after founding, although they disagree on the amount of sales businesses need to have. Some experts say that companies need to have $10 million in sales after five years to be appropriate for angel investment.[49] Others, like Tech Coast Angels, a California–based angel investment group, say that businesses need to have the potential to create at least $50 million in annual revenues to be appropriate for angel financing.[50] Still other experts, like successful and experienced business angel Bill Payne, say that a venture "must have" projected sales of $100 million in year five to be angelappropriate.[51]

A special tabulation of the BITS on the cohort of companies founded in 1996 provides the information needed to determine how many businesses reach each of these sales levels within five to seven years after starting. The BITS is the Census Bureau's effort to match businesses surveyed by the Census at different points in time, and allows a view of the performance of different companies over their first six years of life. According to the BITS, 511,000 new single-establishment businesses were founded in 1996. Of these, 3,608 firms had achieved sales of $10 million or more by 2002; 474 firms had achieved sales of $50 million or more; and 175 firms had achieved sales of $100 million or more.

Angels often say they try to invest in situations in which one out of ten of their investments works out.[52] If this is true, then for the 1996 cohort, the following numbers of companies were appropriate for angel investors to investigate, depending on the angels' targeted sales for portfolio companies after six years of operation: 36,080 firms, if the target is sales of $10 million or more; 4,740 firms, if the target is sales of $50 million or more; and 1,750 firms, if the target is sales of $100 million or more.

THE CHARACTERISTICS OF ANGEL INVESTMENTS

What type of investments do angels make? Several data sources provide information about different dimensions of these investments, including their size, their balance between equity and debt, and their investment terms.

Investment Size

The EUSA data show that the median angel investment made between 2001 and 2003 was $10,000, the mean was $77,000 and the range was $600 to $500,000. (The median and the range are the same if the analysis is restricted to those investors that made an equity investment).

The small size of some of the investments raises the question of whether some of these numbers are errors. Some evidence suggests not. The Angel Investor Performance Project, looked at people affiliated with angel groups, who had a net worth of $10.9 million, had founded an average of 2.7 companies, had been entrepreneurs for an average of 14.5 years, and were among the 13 percent of those contacted willing to talk about their experiences investing in startups. This group reported a range of initial investments of $1,000 to $5 million for the 663 cases for which data were available. If a group of such sophisticated angels reports investments as low as $1,000, then a $600 investment by an investor from a representative sample of angels does not seem incorrect.

Moreover, the median "Series A" equity investment made by highly sophisticated business angels in California for whom the legal work was done by the law firm Brobeck, Phleger & Harrison, was only $27,100.[53] And data from the ACA on the *average* dollar value per round made by an individual angel who was a member of an angel group—all accredited investors— was only $31,457 in 2006.

The GEM data indicate a smaller median investment, with that made over the previous three years by U.S. investors surveyed from 1998 to 2003 being $5,000. For the GEM, no information is available on the number of other investors that invested in the same company as the focal investor or the proportion of these investments that took the form of debt versus equity.

Although the median size of an angel investment taken from the EUSA data might seem low in comparison with some estimates previously gathered, that may be because most studies report the *average* size of angel investments and these investments are highly skewed. In fact, the *average* investment made by angels responding to the EUSA was a much larger $76,774 (in 2003), while the average for the GEM was $47,723 (from 1998-2003).[54] (Restricting the analysis to those investors who made an equity investment yields an EUSA average of $91,826; these data are not available for the GEM). In fact, the EUSA *average* investment size is not that much lower than the *average* size angel investment made by respondents to the CVR Survey—$82,273 in 2003.[55]

Moreover, it is important to note that these are the amounts invested by individual investors, not the amount received by the company in which the investment was made. The respondents also report that the average number of *other* private investors was 3.85 (median was two and the range was zero to 20).[56] Whether these other investors were also angel investors or if they made investments equal to that of the focal angel surveyed is unknown. But if the other investors were angels, then the average investment received per company would be $372,354.

Debt Financing

Angel investing involves the provision of debt as well as equity.[57] In fact, debt accounts for 40.2 percent of the money that angels provide to startups, according to the EUSA.[13] And, according to this same source, 14.8 percent of all angel deals are pure debt. Even among investments in which angels invest in return for some equity, debt is also used approximately 29.8 percent of the time.

Unfortunately, no other current data sources are available to corroborate these data, and the sample size for the EUSA is small. However, the proportion of debt financing shown by the EUSA is not unreasonable by the standards of previous research. Gaston's research on informal investments made in private companies in the 1980s revealed that 41.3 percent of the informal capital provided to companies that had received informal equity investments took the form of debt. This is, in fact, a *higher* proportion of debt than is seen among respondents to the EUSA, which shows that 29 percent of the informal capital provided to businesses in which an informal equity investment was made took the form of debt. This is a *higher* proportion of debt than is seen among angel equity investors who responded to the EUSA. Even among companies that receive informal equity investments, a significant portion of the capital they receive is lent to them.

Investment Instruments

Not much information is available from representative samples of angel investments on the typical investment terms used by angel investors. The only data come from convenience samples of companies known to be backed by sophisticated business angels, which are likely to be biased toward more sophisticated investment instruments. However, even in these samples, equity investments made by business angels are often straight common stock purchases. For instance, one study of sophisticated business angels investing in high-potential companies—the very situation in which convertible preferred stock would be most likely to be used—by Dr. Andrew Wong of the University of Chicago found that common stock was used in 40 percent of investment rounds that involved only angels.[58]

Term Sheet Provisions

Moreover, little data are available from representative samples on the term sheet provisions used by angel investors. The data, again, are from sophisticated angel investors. Nevertheless, the data suggest that relatively little angel investing involves the use of venture capital-like term sheet provisions. First, angel investments are less likely than venture capital investments to use antidilution clauses. Moreover, when sophisticated business angels do use antidilution provisions, the terms of their provisions are much more favorable to entrepreneurs than similar provisions used by venture capitalists. For example, angels use full ratcheting much less frequently than do institutional investors.[59]

Second, angels rarely reserve the right to take actions or change ownership conditional on the entrepreneur's achievement or nonachievement of milestones as venture capitalists do. For instance, one study of investments by sophisticated business angels showed that in only 5 percent of angel investments did investors have a right to force bankruptcy or to veto management decisions. In only 2 percent of angel investments did angels have contingent board rights—rights to obtain control of the board under certain conditions. Warrants at a lower valuation were present in only 4 percent of cases.[60] Furthermore, one study showed that angel investors were statistically less likely than venture capitalists to have made investments in which the shares are redeemable.[61]

Third, angel investment agreements are much less likely than venture capital investment contracts to include a liquidation provision.[62] For example, one study found that only about half of the contracts written by sophisticated accredited angel investors, have a liquidation provision, compared with the vast majority of venture capital contracts.[63] Another study showed that 12 percent of angel only deals had a liquidation preference, compared with 58 percent of venture-capitalist-only deals, a statistically significant difference.[64]

Fourth, most angel investments are made without the angel receiving a seat on the board of directors.[65] One study of investments made by sophisticated business angels showed that board seats were granted in only 42.5 percent of angel funding rounds, and, even then, only the very largest angel investments were sufficient to justify a board seat.[66] Studies of accredited, sophisticated business angels show that only between 15 and 37 percent of them are company directors.[67] Moreover, angels account for only about 18 percent of the board seats among companies that get both angel and venture capital funding. [68]

Follow-on Investment

A minority of business angels make follow on investments. Many studies of sophisticated, well-known, angels show that the typical angel invests in a single round.[69] One study of angels in the United Kingdom found that angels provide follow-on money only 25 percent of the time.[70] Similarly, a study by Professor Rob Wiltbank of Willamette University of a sample of accredited angel investors affiliated with angel groups, and worth an average of $10.9 million, found that only 29 percent of the companies in which angels invest receive follow-on investment.[71]

Investment with Venture Capitalists

Angels and venture capitalists do not invest in the same companies very often. Even among the most sophisticated accredited angel investors, backing the highest potential businesses, studies show that venture capitalist co-investment occurs in only small portion of funding rounds.[72]

Moreover, venture capitalists do not invest in enough businesses for a high rate of angel co-investment to occur, unless the number of angel-backed companies is much smaller than the estimates presented earlier in this report or in earlier studies. According to the National Science Foundation (NSF), in 2004 only 612 companies received venture capital for the seed or start-up phase—the stages at which business angels are likely to have enough capital to co-invest with venture capitalists.[73] If business angels had co-invested with venture capitalists in every one of these companies (a dubious assumption), only 1.1 percent of the 57,300 companies estimated to have received an angel investment that year would have received a co-investment from a business angel and a venture capitalist. Even assuming that business angels co-invest with venture capitalists in all investments that the VCs make, including late-stage ones, the maximum share of companies estimated to have received an angel investment that could also receive a co-investment from a venture capitalist is 4.3 percent.

Valuation

Very few companies that receive angel investments have a multimillion-dollar net worth when they receive angel money. According to the EUSA data, only 36.4 percent of angel investments were made in companies worth more than $1 million at the time of investment.

Data from the 2003 Federal Reserve's Survey of Small Business Finances found that the average net worth of a company less than five years old that had received an informal equity investment in the previous year was $324,000, while the median net worth was $58,000. (The average net worth of all companies that had received an equity investment from a business angel in the previous year was $2.5 million, but the average age of those businesses was 16.5 years and only 15 percent were less than 10 years old, making it difficult to interpret the net worth information on the companies that had received actual angel investments in the previous year)[74].

Of course, it is possible that the valuations angels place on the companies are much higher than their net worth would suggest. The valuation of the typical company that received an external equity investment in its first year of operation can be determined using data from the KFS. The KFS data show that the valuation of a typical firm that was started in 2004 and received an external equity investment in that year was $171,000 (but the average was $1.4 million).

Ownership Share

Business angels rarely obtain majority ownership of their portfolio companies. Most studies show that the angels who invest in the initial financing round of a startup collectively acquire between 20 and 35 percent of the company in which they are investing.[75] For example, a study of a convenience sample of angel investments in 1,377 companies between 2000 and 2004 by the Center for Venture Research at the University of New Hampshire found that the angels took an average of 20.4 percent ownership.[76] The 2003 FRSSBF showed that the first owner of companies less than five years old that received an informal equity investment in the previous 12 months owned 70 percent of the company after the investment occurred. A study of highly sophisticated business angels who made "Series A" investments showed that the average angel owned only 8 percent of angel-backed companies at the pre-Series A stage, and that the average founder still owned 62 percent of his company after an angel-only Series A round was completed.[77]

Exits and Returns

Only a small portion of angel investments has a positive exit. The best financial returns for investors in startup companies tend to come from investments in companies that go public. But only a small portion of angel-backed companies go public. From 1980 through 2006, an average of 264 companies went public in the United States every year. However, many of these were companies in which angels almost certainly do not invest. Approximately 24 percent of the initial public offerings (IPOs) from 2000 through 2006 were buyouts of large long-established companies.[78] A substantial number of the others were foreign companies and companies well in excess of 10 years old. Therefore, the number of companies that angels could potentially have backed that went public was closer to 100 businesses per year.

Estimates from the 2003 FRSSBF show that approximately 50,700 companies per year get angel money. And estimates from the data in the EUSA indicate that 57,300 companies get angel money each year. If 100 angel-backed companies go public each year, that yields an IPO rate of between 0.17 and 0.2 percent of the companies financed by angels, depending on whether the FRSSBF or EUSA data are used to estimate the number of angel-backed businesses.

Few angel investments exit through acquisition. Estimates based on data from the Census Bureau's Longitudinal Establishment and Enterprise Microdata file show that only about 7,000 small businesses are acquired each year.[79] Moreover, only 58 percent of these are 12 years old or younger. Therefore, approximately 4,000 small U.S. businesses less than 13 years old are acquired annually.

Furthermore, the estimate derived from Census data of 4,000+ small, young businesses that are acquired every year might be too high. In 2001, Thomson Financial Securities reported that there were 4,044 mergers and acquisitions worth $5 million or more of businesses of *any* age that were not foreign acquirees, leveraged buyouts, or divestitures.[80] Given the proportion of U.S. businesses under 12 years of age, this suggests that the number of small young companies that are acquired every year for $5 million or more is closer to 2,800.

The numbers are smaller based on the ratio between exits through IPOs and acquisition for venture capitalists. Many observers argue that angels seek follow-on investment from venture capitalists, and that angel financing is only a stage in the process of financing that involves venture capitalists at some point before exit. Because of how this process works, very few companies that receive angel investments will result in an IPO or acquisition without first receiving venture capital. Therefore, the ratio of acquisitions to IPOs for venture capitalists should also hold for business angels. For the 2001 through 2006 period, this ratio averaged 6.7. Given the earlier estimate of 100 angel-backed IPOs every year, this ratio suggests that approximately 670 angel-backed companies are acquired every year. Stated differently, the FRSSBF estimate of the number of angel-backed companies suggests that 1.3 percent of companies that receive angel financing are acquired, whereas the estimate based on EUSA suggests 0.8 percent.

What about returns earned on dollars invested by angels in private companies? Unfortunately, no information is available on the performance of angel investments for a *representative* sample of angel investors. The best we have is data from the FRSCF on the value of a typical *informal equity* investment held by an American household in 2004, which was $79,300 with a cost basis of $47,327. Thus, the multiple on a typical *informal equity* investment held by an American household in 2004 was approximately 1.7.

The lack of studies of the performance of angel investments for a *representative* sample of angel investors necessitates looking at performance data using unrepresentative samples. The best such data are those on the investment performance of business angels affiliated with angel groups, collected by Rob Wiltbank of Willamette University.[81]

It is important to note how unrepresentative the angels in this sample are. Because they are affiliated with angel groups, all of them are accredited investors. Moreover, they have an average net worth of $10.9 million (which, according to the IRS Statistics of Income, puts them in a league with only 123,000 U.S. households), and they made investments in start-ups that averaged $191,000. A full 85 percent of them had at least three years of entrepreneurial experience, and the average angel in the sample had founded 2.7 companies and had been an entrepreneur for 14.5 years.[82] Moreover, participation in Wiltbank's study was voluntary, which almost certainly makes his respondents disproportionately good angel investors.[83]

Wiltbank examined the investment returns of 539 angel investors from 86 groups of angels who had made 3,097 investments, from which they had experienced 1,137 exits. The average investment in the sample (mean investment) generated a profit of $295,000 on an investment of $191,000 in 3.52 years.[84]

However, even these highly successful angels lost money on more than half (52 percent) of their investments. In fact, the median angel investment made by this sample of very experienced and successful angels involved an investment of $50,000 that returned $40,000 or 80 cents on the dollar. Moreover, only 7 percent of the investments accounted for three-quarters of the financial returns.[85]

Many of the investors lost money on their entire portfolio. The data show that almost 40 percent did not get back the money they put into angel investments. And the top 10 percent of investors generated half the financial returns.[86]

Furthermore, properly measuring the rate of return on angel investing requires taking the opportunity cost of the angel's time into consideration, because angel investing is not passive, like putting money into a mutual fund, a venture capital limited partnership, or a hedge fund. The rate of return on angel investments' net of opportunity cost can be found by looking at the data from Wiltbank's study because he measures the amount of time the average angel spends per week on his investments (12 hours). [87] Over the 3.52 years that it takes the average angel investment to reach an outcome, positive or negative, the average angel spends 2,196 hours on his investments. Because the respondents in Wiltbank's sample had an average of 5.16 investments, that comes to 426 hours per venture.

Given the average number of hours put in by an accredited angel to generate the average return, the opportunity cost of the angel's time is $129,520. That is, the angel gave up the opportunity to earn $129,520 in income to generate the financial return from angel investing, money that could have been earned if the angel had invested the money passively.[88] Subtracting this opportunity cost from the amount earned on the typical angel investment yields average angel earnings of $165,480 on a 3.52 year investment of $191,000[32] or an annual rate of return of 19.2 percent. This number is less than the return to investments in venture capital limited partnerships, which, as an asset class, had an average a0-year return of 26.9 percent.[89]

THE RECIPIENTS OF ANGEL INVESTMENTS

Angels invest in a variety of different kinds of companies at a variety of development stages, led by many different types of entrepreneurs in a wide range of industries.

The Industry Distribution of Recipients of Angel Capital

Angels invest in a very wide range of industries. According to the EUSA data, 25 percent of angel investments go into retail businesses, and 12.5 percent go into personal service businesses. And these numbers are not an artifact of the exclusion of investments by "friends" from the angel investment category. The numbers are similar for external equity investments.

The numbers in the SBO for companies aged five-and-under that received external equity investments from 1997 to 2002 show similar patterns. For instance, as Figure 1 shows, the information sector, which includes all of the software companies, accounts for 6.8 percent of the recipients of external equity investments and the professional, scientific and technical services sector 14.4 percent of them, while the retail trade sector accounts for 8.3 percent of them and the wholesale trade sector 9.3 percent.

The data from the KFS, although different from the SBO data, do not indicate a much greater focus on technology companies. The KFS data show that the information sector accounts for 2.5 percent of recipients of external equity investments and the professional, scientific and technical services sector accounts for 9.8 percent of them, while the retail trade sector accounts for 4.9 percent and wholesale trade, 10 percent.

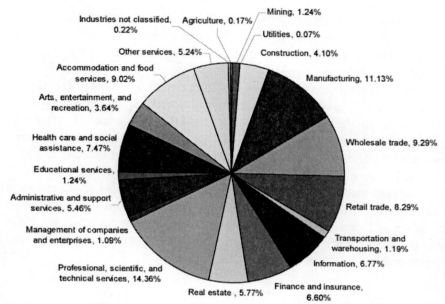

Source: Adapted from a special tabulation of the Survey of Business Owners of the
U.S. Census Bureau.

Figure 1. The Industry Distribution of the Recipients of External Equity Investment,
1997-2002.

Business angels are much less industry-specialized than venture
capitalists.[90] From 1980 through 2004, 81 percent of all venture capital dollars
were invested in just five industries: computer hardware, computer software
(including the Internet), semiconductors and other electronics, communica-
tions, and biotechnology; 73 percent of recipient companies operated in these
industries.[91]

The Age/Stage of Development of Angel-Backed Companies

Angels tend to invest in later-stage companies than many observers
believe. The data from the EUSA show that 64.6 percent of investments made
by angel investors are cashflow-positive, and almost half of the businesses
(48.4 percent) are viewed by the investors as being "established companies" at
the time of investment. Only 35.5 percent of angel investments are made in the
pre-revenue companies.

Furthermore, this is not a function of the businesses to which angels lend money as opposed to those in which they buy shares. The numbers are very similar when the examination is limited to companies that receive an equity investment from business angels.

Similar patterns are seen in the data from the 2003 FRSSBF. The average age of the small businesses that received an informal equity investment in the previous 12 months was 13.3 years. The typical business was 11. Only 45.5 percent of the businesses were under 10 years old. The numbers are even more extreme for businesses that received angel investments, but the sample size is too small to have a great deal of confidence in those numbers.

The seed stage is also not the stage at which most angel group members most like to invest. In fact, slightly more angel groups like early-stage investing—82 percent— compared with 80 percent that favor the seed and start-up stage. Much smaller numbers of angel group members like the expansion (35 percent) or late stages (10 percent).[92]

Characteristics of Angel-Backed Companies

The companies that receive external equity investment are better performing than the typical U.S. startup, but are not necessarily "high-growth potential" companies. The 2003 FRSSBF shows that the typical business of any age—the average age was 13.3 years— that received an *informal equity* investment in the previous year had sales of $435,000, employment of seven, and profits of $7,500.[93]

Although many observers argue that companies need to have a proprietary competitive advantage to receive an angel investment,[94] the data from the KFS indicate that the founders of one of every five businesses that received an external equity investment in their first year of operations (19.2 percent) *do not believe* that their businesses have a competitive advantage of any kind. Moreover, the data from the KFS indicate that only 14.1 percent of the businesses that received an external equity investment in their first year of operation have a patent; 15.5 percent have a copyright; and 33.3 percent have a trademark.

Characteristics of the Owners of Angel-Backed Companies

White male-led businesses account for the vast majority of the companies that receive external equity investments. Data from the SBO showed that only 11 percent of the firms that were five years old or younger and had received external equity investor had a female primary owner.[95] These data also show that only 3.8 percent of businesses that have received external equity investments have a Hispanic primary owner; and only 1.4 percent of those businesses have a Black primary owner.[96]

The patterns are similar for brand new firms. The KFS indicated that 90.4 percent of the primary owners of the businesses that received an outside equity investment from a nonrelative in their first year of operation were White and only 3.6 percent were Black.

The data from the SBO show that middle-aged entrepreneurs receive most of the external equity investments made in this country. More than two-thirds of the entrepreneurs whose businesses had received an external equity investment and were less than six years old in 2002 were between the ages of 35 and 54 years, and only 0.05 percent were younger than 25.[97]

According to the SBO data, two-thirds of the primary owners of the businesses that receive an external equity investment have a college degree or greater education. Similar patterns can be seen in the KFS, which shows that 57.4 percent of the primary owners of the businesses that received an external equity investment in their first year of operation had a college degree or more education.

The data from the KFS show that 60.2 percent of the primary owners of businesses that have received an external equity investment have started at least one prior business. They also show that almost 89.3 percent of the entrepreneurs who founded a business that received an external equity investment in its first year of operation had at least one year of work experience in the industry in which the business was started, and 50.6 percent had more than 10 years of experience.

A large personal investment in a business is not a requirement for the receipt of an external equity investment. The data from the KFS reveal that in 25.5 percent of the businesses in which the founders had invested, the primary owner-founder's combined investment was less than $10,000.

The patterns are similar for the founders' investment of time. According to data from the SBO, the business is the primary source of the founder's income for 54.8 percent of the companies less than six years old that receive an external equity investment. Moreover, the founders of these companies do not put a great deal of time into their businesses. According to the SBO data, in 32.6 percent of the businesses with external equity that are five years old or less, the founder worked 20 hours per week or less on the business, and in the *majority* of the businesses, the founder worked 40 hours per week or less.

RECOMMENDATIONS FOR DATA COLLECTION

One of the problems with understanding angel investment activity has been a paucity of data from large representative samples of angel investors. This lack of data has led researchers to draw inferences from either nonrepresentative convenience samples or small representative samples. The two approaches can both lead to inaccurate estimates (although for different reasons).

An accurate understanding of angel investing requires the creation of large, representative samples of angel investors, angel investments, and angel-financed companies. A large representative sample of angel investors could be created by dramatically increasing the scale of data collection for the EUSA. Increasing the size of the EUSA tenfold would mean that data could be collected from between 200 and 300 business angels, a sample size large enough to draw inferences with confidence.

Better information about angel investments could also be obtained by increasing the scale of data collection for the EUSA, and by expanding the inquiry to all informal investments made in the previous three years, rather than just up to three investments. Alternatively, the SCF could be expanded to collect data from a larger sample and more specific questions about types of informal investments could be added.

Better information about the companies that receive angel investments could be obtained through a dramatic increase (approximately tenfold) in the size of the sample for the FRSSBF. Alternatively, additional questions could be asked in the SBO to identify the source of the external equity investment, as well as more information about the recipient firms.

To get a better understanding of subsets of angel investors, particularly accredited angels, would require new research designs. For instance, to create an adequate sample for the examination of accredited angel investors, an IRS sampling frame on income and net worth would be required to permit high net worth and high income individuals to be oversampled. Otherwise, the sample size necessary to obtain data from a representative sample of several hundred accredited angel investors would need to be close to 500,000 people.

CONCLUSIONS

An Angel investor is a person who provides capital, in the form of debt or equity, from his own funds to a private business owned and operated by someone else who is neither a friend nor a family member.

Based on a review of the literature, a statistical evaluation of data from representative samples of known populations, and a comparison of the results to those from previous studies of nonrepresentative samples of business angels, this study found that:

- The estimated number of people who made an angel investment between 2001 and 2003 was between 331,100 and 629,000 people.
- Between 2001 and 2003, angels invested an estimated $23 billion per year.
- Most angel investors are unaccredited investors, but accredited investors provide the majority of dollars invested.
- The number of companies that receive angel investments annually is between 50,700 and 57,300.
- In 2006, 5,632 angel investors in 128 groups made 947 investments in 512 companies, providing startups with a total of $228.8 million.[98]
- By 2002, 3,608 companies founded in 1996 achieved $10 million or more in sales.
- The typical angel investment made between 2001 and 2003 was $10,000.
- In 2006, the average dollar value invested per angel in an angel group deal was $31,457.
- Debt accounted for 40.2 percent of the money angels provided to startups between 2001 and 2003.
- Between 0.17 and 0.2 percent of the companies financed by angels go public, and between 0.8 and 1.3 percent are acquired.
- The rate of return net of opportunity cost of high-net-worth accredited angels affiliated with groups and willing to talk about their investments is 19.2 percent.
- Between 2001 and 2003, 25 percent of angel investments went into retail businesses and 12.5 percent went into personal service businesses.

- The typical business of any age—the average age was 13.3 years—that received an informal equity investment in the previous year had sales of $435,000, employment of seven, and profits of $7,500.
- Eleven percent of firms that were five years old or younger and had received an external equity investment had a female primary owner; only 3.8 percent had a Hispanic primary owner, and only 1.4 percent had a Black primary owner.
- More than two-thirds of the entrepreneurs whose businesses had received an external equity investment and were less than six years old were between the ages of 35 and 54 years.

Contributions to the Literature

This study contributes to the literature by showing what angel investment activity looks like for representative samples of investors and companies. This information should be useful to researchers seeking to formulate hypotheses and test theories about angel investment activity in the United States.

The study's findings indicate the limitations of previous studies and suggest caution in assuming their validity. The differences between the findings here and those of prior studies that have been based on convenience samples suggest that some of what has been found previously about angel investment activity may be artifacts of the investigation of highly selected samples.

Contributions to Public Policy

This study makes two contributions to public policy analysis. First, it provides more accurate estimates than were previously available of the market and demand for angel capital, the companies that receive angel capital, and angel deals. These data should help policymakers develop ways to enhance the growth of entrepreneurship in the United States. In particular, the data show that the angel capital market is smaller than is often believed and involves more typical types of small business financing than is generally reported. Policy makers need to recognize the true nature of the angel capital market when they make decisions about how to influence this market.

The study provides insight into the investment activity of different groups of angel investors (e.g., accredited and unaccredited investors), which will be useful in predicting how angel investors might respond to public policy. Finally, the study suggests types of policy intervention that could be the most useful in the angel capital market. Because the study shows that most angel investments are not sophisticated equity investments made by accredited investors in high-growth, high-potential startups, policymakers may need to consider more targeted approaches to intervention if they are to influence the financing of companies.

Recommendations for Data Collection

The data on which all discussions of angel investing are based are flawed, leading researchers to draw inferences from either nonrepresentative convenience samples or small representative samples, both of which can lead to inaccurate estimates (although for different reasons.) A truly accurate understanding of angel investing requires data from large representative samples of angel investors, angel investments, and angel-financed companies.

End Notes

[1] Portions of this report will also appear in Scott Shane's book, *Fool's Gold: The Truth Behind Angel Investing in America,* Oxford University Press 2009. Scott Shane is authorized to sign the proposal and to negotiate on the offeror's behalf with the government in connection with this solicitation.

[2] Council on Competitiveness. 2007. *The Competitiveness Index: Where America Stands,* Washington, D.C.: Council on Competitiveness.

[3] Hudson, M. 2007. ACA Briefing and Angel Group Stats. *Presentation to the Angel Capital Association April 12.*

[4] Council on Competitiveness. 2007. *The Competitiveness Index: Where America Stands,* Washington, D.C.: Council on Competitiveness.

[5] The federal securities laws define the term "accredited investor" in Rule 501 of Regulation D as a person whose household net worth exceeds $1 million, or whose income exceeds $200,000 in the two previous years if single (or $300,000 if married) and reasonably expects to maintain the same income level (See Loritz, J. 2007. *Angel Investment: State Strategies to Promote Entrepreneurship and Economic Growth.* National Governors Association Center for Best Practices, Washington, D.C)

[6] Wong, A. 2002. Angel finance: The other venture capital. Working Paper, University of Chicago. The ability to skirt the dicey issue of valuation helps entrepreneurs and angel investors come to an agreement on the financing of new companies, and helps angel investors to avoid making an error in the valuation which will make the business unattractive to venture capitalists in a later round.

[7] Shane, S. 2005. *Angel Investing. A Report Prepared for the Federal Reserve Banks of Atlanta,* Cleveland, Kansas City, Philadelphia, and Richmond. October 1.

[8] Gaston, R. 1989. The scale of informal capital markets. *Small Business Economics,* 1: 223-232.

[9] Benjamin, G., and Margulis, J. 2000. *Angel Financing: How to Find and Invest in Private Equity.* New York: John Wiley and Sons.

[10] Van Osnabrugge, M. 2000. A comparison of business angel and venture capitalist investment procedures: An agency theory-based analysis. *Venture Capital,* 2(2): 91-109.

[11] Wiltbank, R. 2006. At the Individual Level: Outlining Angel Investing in the United States. Downloaded from http://www.willamette.edu/~wiltbank/AtTheIndividualLevel7.pdf

[12] Van Osnabrugge, M. 1998. Do serial and nonserial investors behave differently? An empirical and theoretical analysis. *Entrepreneurship Theory and Practice,* Summer: 23-42

[13] Von Osnabrugge, M., and Robinson, R. 2000. *Angel Investing: Matching Start-up Funds with Start-up Companies – The Guide for Entrepreneurs, Individual Investors, and Venture Capitalists.* San Francisco: Jossey-Bass.

[14] Ibid.

[15] Hill, B., and Power, D. 2002. *Attracting Capital from Angels.* New York: John Wiley and Sons Inc, p.52.

[16] Passive angel investors include both passive investors who co-invest with other active investors and passive investors who invest alone without any active involvement with the portfolio company.

[17] The convergence between the EUSA and GEM data provides some confidence in the accuracy of the population estimates based on them. However, it is difficult to find other sources to corroborate them. The GEM and EUSA data sample the adult-age population and ask about the number of (debt and equity) investments made in the previous three years. Other studies do not sample the adult-age population, do not ask about investment flows, do not include debt as well as equity, and do not look at a three-year period of time. These differences, combined with the examination of different time periods from the EUSA and GEM, mean that the estimates of the number of informal investments from other sources cannot be compared directly to the EUSA and GEM estimates.

[18] Because many angel investors are married in households in which only one individual makes the angel investments, the number of households making angel investments over this period would be lower.

[19] Wright, L. 2004. UNH Center For Venture Research: Angel Investors Have Returned To The Market But The Post Seed Funding Gap Continues. Downloaded from http://unhinfo.unh.edu/news/news_releases/2004/october/lw_20041013cvr.html

[20] To figure out the number of "active" angel investors from the EUSA and the GEM, the EUSA and GEM numbers of people who "made an angel investment in the past three years" are multiplied by the EUSA estimate of the number of angel investments made by each angel (1.27) over the three-year period. Then that number is divided by three (for the number of years). This adjustment yields estimates of 140,000 to 296,000 "active" angel investors in one of the three years covered by the study.

[21] In addition, Several facts suggest the accuracy of these numbers. The EUSA reports that those people who made informal investments over the three-year period made an average of 1.91 of them—a rate of investing almost identical to the 0.68 per year rate found by Robert Gaston in his 1989 study (See Gaston, R. 1989. The scale of informal capital markets. *Small Business Economics,* 1: 223-232.) The rate of informal equity investment is also consistent with data from other sources. Estimates from the EUSA data indicate that 62 percent of informal investments made over this period involved equity. Given that 7.4 million

American adults made informal investments over the three-year period from 2001 to 2003, this suggests that approximately 4.6 million adults made an informal *equity* investment over that time period. These people made 1.91 investments over a three-year period, yielding an estimate of approximately 2.9 million informal equity investments made per person-year from 2001 through 2003. Translated into households, this estimate is approximately 2.2 million. This rate of informal equity investment activity is consistent with that found by other sources. For instance, George Haynes of Montana State University and Charles Ou of the Office of Advocacy of the U.S. Small Business Administration used data from the 1989 through 1998 FRSCF to measure the informal equity *holdings* of U.S. households. They found that in 1998, 1.4 percent of American households *held* an informal equity investment. (See Haynes, G., and Ou, C. 2002. A Profile of Owners and Investors of Privately Held Businesses in the United States, 1989–1998. Paper Presented at the Annual Conference of the Academy of Entrepreneurial and Financial Research, April 25–26, City College of New York.) However, an analysis of the 2004 FRSCF showed a higher proportion of U.S. households with an informal equity holding—1.5 percent. Translated into the number of households, the 2004 FRSCF estimate yields 1.7 million households. That is, estimates from the 2004 FRSCF suggest that U.S. households *hold* approximately 1.7 million informal investments, while estimates from the EUSA suggest that U.S. households *make* 2.2 million informal investments per year.

[22] The EUSA showed that 3.5 percent of the adult-aged population made an informal investment from 2001 to 2003. Because there were 212 million adult Americans in 2003, the estimates from the GEM and EUSA mean that an estimated 7.4 million U.S. adults made an informal investment over this period. The EUSA shows that 8 percent of the informal investments made by U.S. adults during this period were angel investments, yielding 629,000 American adults who made an angel investment over this three-year period. The EUSA shows that the average number of angel investments made by an angel investor over the period was 1.3 and that each investor co-invested with an average of 3.9 investors. Multiplying the 629,000 by 1.3 investments and dividing it by 4.9 investors yields 167,000 companies that received an investment over the three-year period, or an average of 57,300 per year. (These estimates are subject to rounding error.)

[23] These numbers may be imprecisely estimated because they are estimated from small samples.

[24] Angel Investor Market Sustains Modest Recovery in 2004, According to UNH Center for Venture Research. Downloaded from http://www.paangelnetwork.com/index2.php?option= com_ content&do_pdf=1&id=31

[25] It is important to note how much smaller estimates of the number of companies that receive angel investments are than estimates of the number of companies that receive informal investments. Data from the EUSA indicate that 7.4 million people made informal investments from 2001 through 2003. An average of 4.37 investors per company received an informal investment, yielding an average of 564,000 companies per year that received an informal investment. This rate of informal investing is not that different from than that reported in 1989 by Robert Gaston, who found that 9 percent of firms, identified from Dun and Bradstreet files, had received an informal investment (445,600 firms). (Gaston, R. 1989. The scale of informal capital markets. *Small Business Economics*, 1: 223-232.) Moreover, as mentioned earlier in this report, data from the 2003 FRSSBF indicate that 2.6 percent of small businesses received an informal equity investment in the previous 12 months, but for only 7 percent of these businesses (0.2 percent of small businesses overall) was this informal equity investment an angel investment.

[26] Using data from representative samples of the adult-age population of the United States from 2000 to 2004, Paul Reynolds estimates that informal investors provide private companies with $162 billion (in 2004 dollars) annually (see Reynolds, P. Forthcoming. *New Firm Creation in the U.S.: A PSED I Overview*. Berlin: Springer-Verlag; Reynolds, P. 2007. Entrepreneurship in the United States: The Future is Now. Boston: Kluwer.) an amount equal to 1.3 percent of U.S. gross domestic product (GDP). (See Reynolds, P. 2007. *New Firm Creation in the U.S.: A PSED I Overview*. Berlin: Springer-Verlag. The estimate for the amount of informal investment comes from the average amount across the five years reported in Reynolds's study; the venture capital amount is his estimate drawn from other studies. It is important to note that these estimates may be imprecise because some of the money provided by entrepreneurs and informal investors takes the form of debt. However, direct analysis of the EUSA and GEM data from which these estimates are drawn confirms Reynolds's numbers. Comparison of these numbers to estimates reported in previous studies is difficult because few previous studies measure informal investment. However, one study—that published by Robert Gaston in 1989 on investments made in the mid-1980s—can be compared with this one. Gaston found that $32.7 billion of informal equity is invested annually (Gaston, R. 1989. The scale of informal capital markets. *Small Business Economics*, 1: 223-232.) an amount equal to $57.3 billion in 2004 dollars. Because Gaston focused on informal *equity* investments, EUSA data must be adjusted to focus on only informal *equity* investments to compare Gaston's numbers to the EUSA figures. The EUSA data show that 56 percent of informal investment takes the form of debt. Therefore, limiting the EUSA estimate to informal *equity* investments yields annual investments of about $71.3 billion. That is, the EUSA-based estimate for the dollar value of informal equity investments made annually is approximately 24 percent higher than the estimate provided by Gaston.

[27] The median angel investment is $10,000; whereas the median nonangel investment is $5,000. Approximately 8 percent of informal investments were angel investments. Angel investments account for 14.8 percent of the dollar value of the informal investments if the proportion of investments is weighted for the relative sizes of angel and nonangel investments. Since informal investments total $162 billion per year, angel investments amount to about $23 billion per year. The exact proportion of informal investments that are angel investments were used in this calculation. This estimate includes debt provided by business angels. The estimate of only equity provided by business angels every year would be smaller.

[28] The average angel investment is $76,774; the average number of investors per company is 4.85, and the estimated number of companies receiving an angel investment annually is 57,300.

[29] Multiplying the average dollar value of all angel investments made by respondents to the GEM survey in the previous three years ($47,723) by the estimates from the GEM data of the number of people in the United States who made these investments over that period yields an estimate of $32.8 billion over a three-year period, or $10 billion per year. Because there is no information on the number of angel investments made by each investor in the previous three years, the number is assumed to be the same as that found in the EUSA.

[30] Berger, A., and Udell, G. 1998. The economics of small business finance: The roles of private equity and debt markets in the financial growth cycle. *Journal of Banking and Finance*, 22: 613–673.

[31] "The total funds provided to start-ups by the entire U.S. venture capital sector ... was ... $19 billion in 2003." Reynolds, P. 2005. *Entrepreneurship in the United States*. Miami: Florida International University.

[32] Wright, L. 2004. UNH Center For Venture Research: Angel Investors Have Returned To The Market But The Post Seed Funding Gap Continues. Downloaded from http://unhinfo. unh.edu/news/news_releases/2004/october/lw_20041013cvr.html. It is important to note that all of these estimates are smaller than Gaston's estimate of the dollar value of informal equity investment flows made almost 20 years earlier. For instance, the CVR reports angel investment dollars that are only one-third of the $57.3 billion (in 2004 dollars) in annual flows of informal equity investment estimated by Gaston. The gap between these numbers illustrates the importance of distinguishing between *informal equity* and *angel* investment dollars when estimating the size of the angel capital market.

[33] Hudson, M. 1997. ACA briefing and angel group stats. Presentation to the Angel Capital Association, May 24; Becker-Blease, J., and Sohl, J. 2007. Do women-owned businesses have equal access to angel capital? *Journal of Business Venturing*, 22: 503-521; Benjamin, G., and Margulis, J. 2005. *Angel Capital*. New York: Wiley Finance.

[34] Much of what is known about angel groups comes from surveys of the membership of the ACA, which may or may not accurately represent the typical angel group. Almost all well-known angel groups are part of the association, suggesting that the investment numbers for those groups not part of the association are lower, on average, than for those that are members of the ACA.

[35] Hudson, M. 2007. ACA Briefing and Angel Group Stats. Presentation to the Angel Capital Association, April 2. I report the 2006 data because I had access to only the summary statistics for 2007. A number of non-U.S. groups are members of the ACA, which means that the overall numbers need to be adjusted to estimate the U.S. figures. Without access to the raw data, this adjustment was not possible. Moreover, there are some strange numbers reported in 2007, which undermine confidence in the data. For instance, the ACA reports that, in 2007, its member groups were composed of 6,800 angels. However, the association also reports that there were 147 "full member" groups, and 18 "provisional member" groups and that the groups had an average size of 55 people.

[36] Hudson, M. 2007. ACA Briefing and Angel Group Stats. Presentation to the Angel Capital Association April 12.

[37] Hudson, M. 2007. ACA Briefing and Angel Group Stats. Presentation to the Angel Capital Association, April 12.

[38] Angel Capital Association. 2007. *Angel Group Confidence Report*. March 27.

[39] Hudson, M. 2006. Angels, saints and sinners: Where they fit in a community's entrepreneurial finance strategy. Presentation to the CDFA Annual Summit, June 1.

[40] Hudson, M. 2007. ACA Briefing and Angel Group Stats. Presentation to the Angel Capital Association, April 12.

[41] The estimates that follow are likely to be imprecise because the sample size on which they are based is small.

[42] The 23 percent figure represents the percentage of respondents who indicated that they are not accredited investors and who made an angel investment in the previous three years. The respondents who made an angel investment in the previous three years could have identified up to three informal investments, of which one, two, or three could have been angel investments. The 21 percent refers to the angel percentage of the total number of reported informal investments made by someone who made at least one angel investment over the three-year period and who was an unaccredited investor. The 2 percent difference between

the two numbers reflects a slightly higher tendency for accredited investors to have made more than one angel investment in the past three years than for unaccredited investors to have done so..

[43] The $200,000 cutoff understates the proportion of credit users whose incomes would make them unaccredited investors because many people who received the angel tax credit are likely to be married.

[44] Wisconsin Department of Revenue, Division of Research and Policy. 2007. *Individual Income Tax Statistics Report for Tax Year 2005*, Madison, WI.: Wisconsin Department of Revenue

[45] Benjamin, G., and Margulis, J. 2000. *Angel Financing: How to Find and Invest in Private Equity*. New York: John Wiley and Sons.

[46] Reynolds, P. 2004. *Entrepreneurship in the United States Assessment*. Miami, FL: Florida International University Limited liability companies are included among companies that take the appropriate legal form for angel investments.

[47] May, J., and Simmons, C. 2001. *Every Business Needs an Angel*. New York: Crown Books

[48] Fenn, G., and Liang, N. 1998. New resources and new ideas: Private equity for small businesses. *Journal of Banking and Finance*, 22: 1077–1084

[49] Sohl, J. 1999. The early-stage equity market in the USA. *Venture Capital*, 1(2): 101–120.

[50] Downloaded from http://www.techcoastangels.com/Public/Content.aspx?ID=EA6BF3BE-964F-11D4- AD7900A0C95C1653&Redir=False

[51] Payne, B. Engaging Angel Investors. Downloaded from http://www.eventuring.com/eShip/appmanager/eVenturing/eVenturingDesktop?_nfpb=true&_pageLabel=eShip_linkDetail&_nfls=false&id=Entrepreneurship/Resource/Resource_546.htm&_fromSearch=false&_nfl s=false.

[52] Villalobos, L., and Payne, B. 2007. Valuation of Seed/Start-up Ventures. Presentation to the Power of Angel Investing Seminar.

[53] Goldfarb, B., Hoberg, G., Kirsch D., and Triantis, A. 2007. Are angels preferred venture investors? Working Paper, University of Maryland. Brobeck, Phleger & Harrison is no longer in operation.

[54] If some sort of bias led the mean and median size of an angel investment from the EUSA to be too low, then the average size angel investment of angel group members would be expected to be larger, not smaller, than the average size of an investment from a respondent to the EUSA. All angel group members are accredited investors, while only 28 percent of angels in the EUSA are accredited investors. Because accredited investors are wealthier and have higher incomes, on average, than unaccredited investors, one would expect the average investment by accredited investors to be larger than the average investment by unaccredited investors. Therefore, it is unlikely that the EUSA estimate of the median investment for angel investors would be too low.

[55] Center for Venture Research. 2007. The Angel Investor Market in 2006 downloaded from http://unhinfo.unh.edu/news/docs/2006angelmarketanalysis.pdf

[56] Restricting the analysis to those investors that made an equity investment yields an average number of four coinvestors, while the median remains two. For the Angel Investor Performance Project, the range is zero to 12, the mean is 5.2 and the median is two.

[57] Angel investors may extend only loans to the businesses that they finance and take no ownership stake.

[58] Wong, A. 2002. Angel finance: The other venture capital. Working Paper, University of Chicago.

[59] Ibid.

[60] Ibid.

[61] Goldfarb, B., Hoberg, G., Kirsch D., and Triantis, A. 2007. Are angels preferred venture investors? Working Paper, University of Maryland.

[62] Amis, D., and Stevenson, H. 2001. *Winning Angels*. London: Pearson Education.

[63] Von Osnabrugge, M., and Robinson, R. 2000. *Angel Investing: Matching Start-up Funds with Start-up Companies – The Guide for Entrepreneurs, Individual Investors, and Venture Capitalists*. San Francisco: Jossey-Bass.

[64] Goldfarb, B., Hoberg, G., Kirsch D., and Triantis, A. 2007. Are angels preferred venture investors? Working Paper, University of Maryland.

[65] Benjamin, G., and Margulis, J. 2001. *The Angel Investor's Handbook*. Princeton, NJ: Bloomberg Press.

[66] Wong, A. 2002. Angel finance: The other venture capital. Working Paper, University of Chicago.

[67] Von Osnabrugge, M., and Robinson, R. 2000. *Angel Investing: Matching Start-up Funds with Start-up Companies – The Guide for Entrepreneurs, Individual Investors, and Venture Capitalists*. San Francisco: Jossey-Bass.

[68] Wong, A. 2002. Angel finance: The other venture capital. Working Paper, University of Chicago.

[69] Hill, B., and Power, D. 2002. *Attracting Capital from Angels*. New York: John Wiley and Sons Inc.; Von Osnabrugge, M., and Robinson, R. 2000. *Angel Investing: Matching Start-up Funds with Start-up Companies – The Guide for Entrepreneurs, Individual Investors, and Venture Capitalists*. San Francisco: Jossey-Bass.

[70] Mason, C., and Harrison, R. 1996. Informal venture capital: A study of the investment process, the post-investment experience and investment performance. *Entrepreneurship and Regional Development*, 8: 105- 125.

[71] Wiltbank, R., and Boeker, W. 2007. Returns to Angel Investors in Groups, Working Paper, Ewing Marion Kauffman Foundation.

[72] Wong, A. 2002. Angel finance: The other venture capital. Working Paper, University of Chicago.

[73] The data were downloaded from http://www.nsf.gov/statistics

[74] These numbers are likely to be imprecisely estimated because the sample on which they are estimated is very small.

[75] Wainwright, F., and Groeninger, A. 2005. *Note on Angel Investing*, Tuck School of Business Administration at Dartmouth Center for Private Equity and Entrepreneurship, Case Number 5-0001; Benjamin, G., and Margulis, J. 2000. *Angel Financing: How to Find and Invest in Private Equity*. New York: John Wiley and Sons; Wong, A. 2002. Angel finance: The other venture capital. Working Paper, University of Chicago; Sohl, J. and Sommer, B. 2007. Angel investing: changing strategies during volatile times. Working Paper, Center for Venture Research, University of New Hampshire; Van Osnabrugge, M. 2000. A comparison of business angel and venture capitalist investment procedures: An agency theory-based analysis. *Venture Capital*, 2(2): 91-109; Coveney, P., and Moore, K. 1998. *Business Angels*, New York: John Wiley.

[76] Becker-Blease, J., and Sohl, J. 2007. Do women-owned businesses have equal access to angel capital? *Journal of Business Venturing*, 22: 503-521.

[77] Goldfarb, B., Hoberg, G., Kirsch D., and Triantis, A. 2007. Are angels preferred venture investors? Working Paper, University of Maryland.

[78] Calculated from data downloaded from http://bear.cba.ufl.edu/ritter/New%20Folder/ IPOs2006 Factoids.pdf

[79] Office of Advocacy. 1998. Mergers and Acquisitions in the United States, 1990-1994. Downloaded from http://www.sba.gov/ADVO/stats/m_a.html

[80] See http://www.census.gov/prod/2003pubs/02statab/business.pdf

[81] Prior to Professor Wiltbank's effort, there were other studies of the performance of angel investment efforts. One study looked at 1,200 angel investors' liquidated investments and found that over an average of eight years, 39 percent lost money, 19 percent broke even, 30 percent generated more than a 50 percent IRR and 12 percent generated more than 100 percent IRR. (See Benjamin, G., and Margulis, J. 2001. *The Angel Investor's Handbook*. Princeton, NJ: Bloomberg Press.) Another study of 128 exited investments made by 51 business angels in the United Kingdom found that 34 percent lost all the investment, 13 percent returned only as much as the capital, 23 percent had a return of more than 50 percent and only 10 percent generate more than 100 percent. (See Mason, C., and Harrison, R. 1999. The rates of return from informal venture capital investments: Some UK evidence. Paper Presented at the Babson College-Kauffman Foundation Entrepreneurship Research Conference, University of South Carolina, May 12-15.) However, these studies are less well designed than Professor Wiltbank's study, which makes the results that they provide less likely to be accurate.

[82] Wiltbank, R., and Boeker, W. 2007. Returns to Angel Investors in Groups, Working Paper, Ewing Marion Kauffman Foundation.

[83] People with worse performance are less likely to participate in the study.

[84] Wiltbank, R., and Boeker, W. 2007. Angel Performance Project. Presentation to the Kauffman Foundation Conference on Entrepreneurship and Innovation Data, November 2.

[85] Wiltbank, R., and Boeker, W. 2007. Returns to Angel Investors in Groups, Working Paper, Ewing Marion Kauffman Foundation.

[86] Wiltbank, R., and Boeker, W. 2007. Returns to Angel Investors in Groups, Working Paper, Ewing Marion Kauffman Foundation.

[87] http://www.willamette.edu/~wiltbank/AtTheIndividualLevel7.pdf

[88] Because all of the angel investors in Wiltbank's sample are accredited investors, it is possible to estimate the cost to them of spending 426 hours on a venture. The minimum income level to meet SEC accreditation requirements is $200,000 per year for a single person, which can be used as a conservative estimate of minimum annual income of someone in the sample. IRS data show that the average adjusted gross income of people who earn more than $200,000 per year was $608,545 in 2005. (Calculated from data downloaded from http://www.irs.gov/ taxstats/indtaxstats/article/0,,id=96981,00.html). Assuming that people who earn $608,545 per year work an average of 40 hours per week and take two weeks of vacation per year, the opportunity cost of an accredited angel's time is estimated conservatively at $304.27 per hour. (Readers should note that this is a very conservative estimate. The typical angel is married. Therefore, most of the angels in the sample would have to exceed $300,000 per year in income to meet SEC accreditation requirements. Moreover, the respondents have an average net worth of $10.9 million. People with an average net worth that high probably have incomes considerably higher than $200,000 per year.)

[89] For the period ending in September 2004. See http://www.prnewswire.com/cgi-bin/stories.pl?ACCT=109&STORY=/www/story/01-19-2005/0002862967&EDATE.

[90] Van Osnabrugge, M. 2000. A comparison of business angel and venture capitalist investment procedures: An agency theory-based analysis. *Venture Capital*, 2(2): 91-109.

[91] Calculated from data downloaded from http://www.nsf.gov/statistics

[92] Hudson, M. 2007. ACA Briefing and Angel Group Stats. Presentation to the Angel Capital Association April 12.

[93] These estimates are likely to be imprecise because the sample on which they are estimated is very small.

[94] Benjamin, G., and Margulis, J. 2001. *The Angel Investor's Handbook*. Princeton, NJ: Bloomberg Press; Payne, B. Engaging Angel Investors. Downloaded from http://www.eventuring.com/
eShip/appmanager/eVenturing/eVenturingDesktop?_nfpb=true&_pageLabel=e
Ship_linkDetail&_nfls=false&id=Entrepreneurship/Resource/Resource_546.htm&_fromSe
arch=false&_nfl s=false.

[95] Calculated from data downloaded from http://www.census.gov/prod/ec02/sb0200cscbt.pdf

[96] Ibid.

[97] Calculated from data downloaded from http://www.census.gov/csd/sbo/cbosummary
offindings.htm.

[98] Hudson, M. 2007. ACA Briefing and Angel Group Stats. Presentation to the Angel Capital Association April 12.

INDEX

D

E

F

loans, 78
logit analyses, 18

M

majority, 35, 37, 61, 63, 69, 70, 71
malfeasance, 56
management, 14, 15, 20, 22, 24, 60
mapping, 18
market segment, 31
market share, 13, 27
marketing, 9, 26, 31
Maryland, 78, 79
matrix, 17
median, 53, 54, 58, 59, 62, 65, 76, 78
medical, 5, 28, 30
medical expertise, 5, 28
medicine, 5
membership, 77
memory, 11
mental model, 9
mental processes, 8, 9
mental state, 8
mergers, 64
methodology, 29
Miami, 77, 78
models, 7, 9, 10, 11, 12, 16, 30
Montana, 75
multidimensional, 11, 15
multiple regression, 31

N

nonfunded business plans, 3, 17, 18, 19, 20, 21

O

Office of Advocacy, 1, 3, 33, 75, 80
officials, 1, 33
operations, 68
ownership, 50, 60, 63, 78

P

participants, 10, 13, 14
pattern recognition, 28
pedagogy, 22, 23
peer review, 3
performers, 5
permit, 70
personal contact, 14
Philadelphia, 46, 74
policy, 39, 72, 73
policymakers, 39, 45, 72, 73
population, vii, 34, 36, 39, 42, 43, 45, 46, 48, 51, 54, 74, 75, 76
portfolio, 57, 63, 65, 74
preparation, iv
primary data, 45
principal component analysis, 17
principal components analysis (PCA), 17
probability, 19, 31
probability distribution, 31
problem solving, 5, 11
profit, 15, 46, 50, 65
PRO-FIT, 12, 15, 18, 19, 20, 31
profit margin, 15
profitability, 14
property rights, 15
psychology, 11
public policy, 39, 72, 73

Q

qualitative research, 45

R

random errors, 10
rate of return, 35, 38, 65, 66, 71
reality, 10
reasoning, 5, 9, 30
recognition, 28